My Fight For

The Mega

Acknowledgements

I would like to thank Patricia, Hilary and Rachel for their help and assistance in preparing this book; it is greatly appreciated.

First Printing, 2016

ISBN 978-1522987413

www.themegapigfile.co.uk

This is a true story drawn from my real experience, notes I made at the time, and from memories that will last a lifetime. No events have been consciously added to increase the impact of my story, although some descriptions and dialogue have been added to help the reader to understand and appreciate our situation. I have been advised to change the names of people and places in this book, for legal reasons.

They said we abused our children.

They said we colluded to deceive professionals.

They said we distorted facts, past and present.

They said they had to deal with scum like me every day of the week.

They named our case file **"Mega Pig"**.

My Fight For My Family

I would like to start by telling you my reason for writing this book. My daughters asked me to write down all the things they were too young to remember. I'd told them bits of what happened to our family – how we were pulled into the secretive, shadowy world of social services and the child protection team. But they wanted to know in detail. So, this is what happened when the truth became worthless; when reasoning lost its meaning and when lies and deception became the norm.

Chapter 1

To begin my story, we must go back to 1985, when I was 33 years old, living with my parents; while my girlfriend, Martha, was 23 and shared a flat with her sister.

I had just started my own business, which was occupying a lot of my time. Martha was pregnant, and – although we did not know it at the time – in her medical notes from one antenatal visit, the doctor noted that she appeared to be a very level-headed and sensible young woman.

In **September 1985,** when Martha was eight months pregnant with our baby, Sally, she was allocated a ground floor bedsit in Primmers Lane, Bankham. She was thrilled to have somewhere of her own, but soon, the upstairs neighbour's behaviour took the shine off.

On **14 October 1985**, Sally was born, which was amazing. Martha returned to the bedsit and I sat on the sofa next to Martha, gazing at Sally in her arms; her perfect starfish fingers grasping my fingertip. I marvelled at her tiny fingernails. I couldn't stop grinning, to think that this beautiful baby was mine - a part of me – and Martha. My own family!

Then a loud 'CLUNK' shook the ceiling, and Martha and I glanced up. A scuffling sound came from the flat above, and we clearly heard raised voices.

"YA BITCH! YA BITCH!" A loud, deep shout rang out, interspersed with high-pitched shrieking and whimpering.

Martha and I were frozen. We looked at one another, eyes wide.

"What the hell's that?" I whispered. "A domestic?"

"I dunno," Martha said, her eyes glistening, close to tears. "It happens all the time. Through the night, too."

She gave out a soft sigh, heavy with sadness. I noticed the dark shadows under her eyes.

The flats where Martha lived were converted houses, so the soundproofing was minimal. Not only could you hear the neighbours talking and walking, you even heard them urinating or their solid waste splashing into the toilet bowl before clearly hearing them flush the toilet. That was just normal life – let alone the excessive noise from upstairs.

3

To begin with, we thought there was more than one person in the upstairs flat, but we eventually realised that it was just one man, talking and shouting to himself, using different voices. It was quite scary at times. It turned out that the flat above was occupied by a schizophrenic. For days and nights at a time, he would play excessively loud music or stamp about, continuous banging, screaming and shouting in different voices.

Martha complained to the council and the police, but they said nothing could be done because of the neighbour's psychological condition. With all that was happening in the flat above and the fact that she had just had a baby – unable to gain sufficient sleep, Martha soon became very tired and run-down. Most days, just to get away from the noise from the flat above, she would wash, change and feed Sally, and then they would go and spend time in the shopping precinct in the town centre, sitting on one of the seats, when it was warm.

But she couldn't do that all day, every day, and life in the bedsit was torture. My circumstances meant that she couldn't live with me at my parents' house, and I didn't have any money for us to live together anywhere else. I was desperately working all hours, trying to establish my business and get some money for us to be a family. But I was earning nothing to speak of, while working too hard. Meanwhile, Martha was suffering. Being a young mother is bad enough, but sadly, I couldn't support her, either. And what chance did she get to relax, with someone playing loud music and screaming all night long? The whole set-up was awful. The road the flats were on was also well known in the area for drug use. Everything felt unsafe; Martha's nerves were on edge all the time, from exhaustion. I was worried for Martha and for our baby, but I didn't know what to do.

I'd told various members of my family what was happening. My then sister-in-law, Ruth, suggested I contact Social Services and ask for their help in finding somewhere better for Martha to live.

I had never had any dealings with Social Services – I didn't even know their telephone number – so Ruth offered to call them for me. I mentioned this to Martha.

"Don't you dare!" she said.

"Why? What?"

"Social workers only cause problems!" she snarled, almost delirious with tiredness.

"How do you know?"

"I've heard. Common knowledge. Don't ring them. Get the Social involved, they interfere."

Looking at her sad, worn face and red eyes; oppressed by the thudding and screaming that I could escape, and after dodging the spaced-out guys staggering in the road and the crack-dealer looming in the shadows, I felt that some interference was needed. I was helpless myself, and Martha and Sally needed far more help than I could give. I could see Martha wasting away before my eyes, under this stress. She just needed somewhere better to live! In spite of Martha begging me not to contact Social Services, I told my sister-in-law to phone them, anyway.

On **12 December 1985,** Ruth phoned Social Services on my behalf, to express my concerns about Martha and Sally's welfare, since by then, Martha appeared to be in a very run-down state. Later that day, a social worker called me while I was at work and said they were at Martha's bedsit, but she wouldn't open the door to them. They asked if I had a key and, if so, could I come and let them in so they could talk to her.

"Yeah," I said, grabbing my coat. "Yeah. I'll be there, soon as I can."

When I arrived, there were two social

workers standing outside, looking annoyed. I clearly remember one of the social workers, whose name was Deborah Smith, because I recognised her from my school days. She had been in the year above me. She didn't acknowledge me, except to say, "Have you got the key?"

I unlocked the bedsit door, to find Martha in her coat, just about to leave with Sally in her pram.

"The social workers just want to talk about your housing needs," I told her, as she pushed past me, out of the door. She was fuming and could barely look at me, let alone the social workers. I could understand. After all, I'd gone against her wishes, while they were complete strangers and she hadn't even been expecting them.

"Not talking to them. Going out. Into town."

She ignored the social workers outside and began to push the pram off the front step, onto the pavement.

"You're not going anywhere until you talk to us!" Deborah Smith cried, stepping in front of the pram, barring her way. She grabbed hold of the pram handle and held on, to prevent Martha from leaving.

"Get off!" Martha growled, and they wrestled with the pram, pushing and shoving it. The other social worker joined in; Martha trying to head it towards town and the social workers attempting to turn the pram around, back inside the house.

"Get off!" Martha cried. "Get lost, you cow! Stop it!"

The two social workers just held the pram fast between them, so it couldn't be moved. I was frozen, appalled. I wanted Martha to speak to them, to get help, so I felt I couldn't intervene against them and back her up, but I didn't like what I was seeing.

"Go away!" Martha roared, and then began shouting at them loudly, swearing and becoming increasingly agitated. It was clear that she was feeling very threatened by their actions, by then. I stood paralysed in horror, not knowing what to do for the best. At the time, I couldn't think, but it all felt wrong – like overkill. The fact that they physically stopped her and grabbed the pram, and it looked so violent – that was the worst! But little did I know – the worst was yet to come.

On reflection, I don't understand why they didn't let her walk and relax, as she wanted to. They could easily have walked beside her and spoken to her, but there seemed to be no empathy from them: their tone was stern and firm and seemed to convey an attitude of superiority, to me.

With all the shouting and jostling of the pram, Sally was awake and began crying, so Martha picked her up out of the pram.

"Don't let her get away!" Deborah Smith shouted and the other social worker lunged forward, trying to hold Martha's arms – and a struggle ensued.

Smith reached to pull Sally away from Martha's embrace, while Martha elbowed her away with a grunt. Smith gasped, her face furious.

"Oh…" I ventured, putting out one hand, helplessly. "Hey, now!"

I was seriously concerned that Sally could be hurt and astonished by the actions of the social workers. It was as though they had decided to get their hands on Sally, whatever the cost.

Martha was no seven-stone lightweight. Had she not been holding onto Sally, I am quite sure she could have floored both social workers with little problem, but her main aim was to get away from them, with Sally still protectively in her arms. But the two social workers together – one peeling Martha's fingers off Sally's clothing by digging her fingernails deeply into Martha's skin – finally wrenched a wailing Sally out of Martha's grasp.

Bereft and in despair, Martha gave a heart-rending shriek and ran off towards the town centre, crying hysterically.

I stood open-mouthed; horrified. I could not believe what I had just witnessed!

The social workers had only come to talk about the housing situation and it had ended up with Martha having Sally forcibly removed from her! "Snatched" was more appropriate.

I held out my hands for my crying baby daughter. "I'll take Sally to my parents'," I said. "Then, I'll come back and wait for Martha to come home."

"That's not possible," Smith replied. "Martha's gone. She's legally deserted her child."

"What?" I thought she was joking for a minute, but her face said otherwise. "Sally hasn't been deserted!" I cried. "I'm here! I'm her father!"

Smith sternly informed me: "You're not married to Sally's mother, so you have no legal right to Sally."

"But – that's..."

"The baby will have to come with us," Smith interrupted. "We'll contact you later."

"But – wait! That's not..."

And off they went, taking Sally with them. I

was reeling. Only through the shock of what had just happened and my belief that they must be right – they knew the law better than I did – did I go along with it. I went in and waited in Martha's bedsit, my head in my hands. This was not going the way I'd imagined. But still – when Martha came back, Social Services would bring Sally back, and we could sort this all out. I reckoned.

Looking back now, I still cannot agree with Deborah Smith's assertion that Martha's running off constituted desertion. If you leave your child with friends or the childminder, is that desertion? How can a child have been deserted when it's with its father? I feel that Smith twisted the meaning of the law when she said I had no rights because I wasn't married to the baby's mother, which meant the baby had been deserted. Smith didn't seem to consider the fact that Martha hadn't just upped and left the baby: the social workers had forcibly removed Sally from her, in the street! And for no reason – other than Martha not wanting to talk to them about the housing situation! How would that stand, legally?

Martha returned about half an hour later, breathless and wary. She looked around the room.

"Where's Sally?"

She naturally expected Sally to be with me. I explained what the social workers had said.

"What? You just let them take her?" she said, her lower lip trembling.

"It's OK. Only while you were gone. They said they'll be in touch. They'll bring her back."

We waited for them to return, as they said they would. Martha's agitation had used all her remaining energy, and she was weak and washed out.

When they finally returned, it was without Sally.

Deborah Smith said they had obtained a Place of Safety order, due to Martha's desertion of Sally.

"I didn't desert her!" Martha said weakly. "You took her!"

"Where is she?" I asked

Smith continued: "Sally is being examined by a doctor and will then be taken to foster carers."

"Foster carers?" I gasped. "There's no need for that!"

They showed us a copy of the Place of Safety order and I stared blankly at the piece of paper.

"This isn't valid," I informed them. "You've

used the wrong surname for Sally. They had put Martha's name on the order, but on Sally's birth certificate, she has my surname.

"It doesn't matter whose name is on the order," Smith said.

They left us childless. Martha was too wiped out and numb to even cry. I stayed the night and held her close, while the screaming and clattering upstairs filled the void.

Chapter 2

The following day the social workers said we could visit Sally at the foster parents' house, which we did. Martha tried to raise a smile when she saw our baby, but most of the time, she wept, rocking back and forth with Sally in her arms.

We were also informed that an interim care order would be applied for. Martha sat, defeated and silent for much of the time.

A week or so later, as we waited in court for the hearing, the child protection worker, Sharon Daily, asked if we would be opposing the care order. I told her that we would.

"I strongly advise you against this," she said. "We've received medical reports that show Sally has suffered very serious physical injuries, including fractured bones, an old fracture and internal ruptures."

"What?" I said, incredulous. My mouth was dry, and I looked questioningly at Martha, whose face was white and frozen.

"The report also states that during a previous meeting with Martha, she confessed to inflicting them – punching her."

I gasped aloud, but Martha just looked completely blank and slightly bewildered. *What the hell?* I went cold and my head buzzed. Who was this woman I thought I knew? Had the noise and stress tipped Martha further over the edge than I'd imagined?

Daily told us that if we opposed the care order, newspaper reporters would be allowed into the court, meaning that our names would then be made public.

"And you know – the public take a low view of people who do this sort of thing to babies," she warned. "Your lives – well... It would be terrible for all of you."

I only later found out that family courts are private and the media are never allowed access to them. Clearly, right from the outset, the social workers were prepared to use untruths to get their own way.

At this time, I had no reason not to believe Sharon Daily, since she even claimed they had doctors' reports and x-rays confirming the injuries. Even so, I found it hard to believe that Martha would have done such a thing. We were actually never shown any of this evidence. But in that moment, I had no reason to doubt her. It was unbelievable that the authorities would make up a story like this.

Still, I was in a state of shock after these allegations had been sprung on us and I was horrified that Martha could be guilty. Clearly, Sally had to be protected and I was also terrified of the media attention and potential attacks Daily had threatened would happen, once our identities were made public; so, for the best, I agreed not to oppose the interim care order. Martha was in no fit state to make any decisions, although she numbly nodded her agreement.

Without any opposition from us, the order was granted.

After the interim care order was granted, we were told that social services would now proceed towards obtaining a full care order and that this court hearing would be on **15 February 1986**. I decided that I would not oppose the full care order. Martha continually denied having hurt Sally, but with doctors' reports and x-rays telling a different story, how could I go against social services? When you have been told that your young child has suffered these sorts of injuries, it rather knocks the stuffing out of you. Especially when your partner is to blame. My blood ran cold at the thought.

Quietly, at home, much later, I asked Martha what they meant when they said she'd confessed to inflicting the injuries.

"I never said I hurt Sally," she mumbled.

"Can you remember exactly what you did say to the social workers?"

"Well, they asked if I considered myself a little heavy-handed at times," Martha murmured. She looked at her chunky hands, slowly flexing her broad fingers. "Well, obviously I'm not petite or graceful. I can be clumsy. So, I said yes."

They also asked if she had ever laid Sally down quickly, to which Martha also answered yes.

The social worker had then asked her, "Do you think someone who was not heavy-handed might consider the way you put Sally down quickly as, a bit like 'throwing her down'?"

And Martha had frowned, but, imagining slender ladies with fragile little hands slowly and carefully laying down a baby, she admitted that she supposed that they might do.

This is what social services had taken to be Martha's confession to inflicting serious injuries on Sally by hitting her with clenched fists!

At the time, it did not cross my mind, but if Sally indeed had suffered these serious injuries –

and if Martha had confessed to causing them by beating Sally with clenched fists, surely the police would have become involved? To cause such injuries to a baby is, of course, a serious criminal offence. And yet there was never any police involvement, whatsoever. But at the time, I lived in fear. I respected authority, and, taking their word for it, I doubted Martha.

Martha and I attended the court hearing for the full care order, which was heard by three magistrates who had viewed the social services reports. I remember the social services solicitor talking to the magistrates, but I don't recall what was said. Words were being spoken but I could not process them; my mind was numb and hazy. I must have realised that the full care order was inevitable. I do recall the magistrate seated in the central position looking at us in what I interpreted as disgust. A female magistrate, seated on the left, leant over and began talking quietly to the central magistrate and then the three magistrates were talking between themselves. The court clerk said that the magistrates were leaving the room for a while to discuss the case.

On their return to the courtroom, the central

magistrate, who appeared to be the most senior, the one that had given us unpleasant looks, spoke, "My fellow magistrate has several concerns as to the validity of the injury claims..."

I glanced at Martha, who muttered, "What's that mean?"

I shrugged. But if a magistrate was sceptical, it seemed to me that there was something not quite right about social services' accusations against Martha.

In that moment, the atmosphere changed. I noticed that the central magistrate was no longer looking at Martha with disgust, but apparently with serious concern. It was as if a fog had lifted: my mind cleared and my thoughts became focused. But Martha still had her head down and was staring at the floor.

The magistrate seated on the left, who had initially leant over to urgently talk to the other two before they left the room – began to speak.

"As a recently retired surgeon, I have a professional medical background," the magistrate stated. "And while I am aware of the seriousness of the alleged injuries, I have serious doubts about the social services report," she told the social workers.

The social workers shifted in their seats,

leaning in towards one another, muttering urgently.

The magistrate asked the social services personnel to clarify several things to her. "Your report claims that Martha confessed to beating the baby on several occasions using her clenched fists and that this brought about the injuries described in this report: an old fracture of a rib and current fractures to the legs are referred to, and also a internal rupture..."

The social workers looked shiftily at one another. One of them covered her mouth with her hand, then started biting her thumbnail, staring wide-eyed at the magistrate.

The magistrate went on: "And yet, how could there be an 'old fracture' in an eight-week-old baby? Fractures only heal completely after a number of months. Such an injury would be older than the baby itself! Can you explain that?"

Sharon Daily, the social worker, took a visible intake of breath, her shoulders tense. "No."

"And how could there be current fractures – but no mention of trauma? That is, bruising of the skin?" She asserted that through her medical experience she knew that babies' bones are supple and to cause fractures by beating a baby with clenched fists would almost certainly leave severe trauma and visible bruising.

"And this 'internal rupture'. What, precisely, had ruptured? Can you give details? Say what the rupture was?"

A white-faced Sharon Daily looked totally shocked and turned to another social worker, who I believed to be her team leader. After a brief animated conversation between them, Daily told the court. "I don't know."

"You cannot provide any explanation for any of these discrepancies? " The magistrate paused, haughtily, then said, "If this baby had been beaten in such a way as to cause the severe injuries stated in the report, how could the baby be allowed to go straight to foster parents, as your report states, and not be detained in hospital? And no hospital would have released such a young baby with the sort of injuries your reports describe."

Again, Sharon Daily turned to someone else for guidance before answering that she did not know. From their fidgeting and agitation, it seemed like the social workers were in complete turmoil, that they had not expected this sort of response from the court.

Sharon Daily was then asked, "In your report, it states that the baby is now thriving, but

21

with the injuries stated and without hospitalisation, how can this be?"

Her head hanging, once more, Daily responded that she did not know.

"Do you think a mistake has been made in the case?"

Daily indicated that she did not.

The magistrate then asked to see the x-ray report, but after a brief exchange of words between the social workers, Daily informed the magistrate that they did not have a copy.

"Can I see the doctor's report?" the magistrate then asked.

"We don't have a copy of that," Daily said.

"Then, can you give us the name of the doctor who carried out the examination?"

"We don't have it."

"You have, in fact… no evidence at all?"

The magistrates looked from one to the other. Even I could tell that there was something fishy going on, by now.

I later discovered that there had been some sort of doctor's report and even a report on an x-ray, but it seemed that once they discovered that this magistrate had a medical background, the social services personnel did not dare show her the reports.

I saw those reports some years later and I could see why the social workers kept them from the magistrate, but I will get to that later.

The magistrate asked social services how their report had come about without any form of evidence available.

The social workers put their heads together for several minutes, talking urgently, and then Sharon Daily said, "A colleague overheard doctors discussing a case and assumed they were discussing Sally."

"What? I cannot accept this!" the magistrate bellowed, as she rose from her seat and slammed the report down on the table. Her eyes flamed with anger.

The other magistrates agreed. The guardian ad litem, a social worker whose purpose is to represent the child, immediately stood up and stated that because of Sally's age, mother and baby must be reunited as soon as possible

"But because of Martha's housing conditions, she must not be allowed to take Sally back to the bedsit. I recommend that social services contact the Bankham housing department immediately, so that suitable housing can be found for them."

The magistrate was aware of the housing situation, concerned that Sally needed to be living in better conditions, and said she would grant a care order– provided that neither parent objected, so that Sally could be looked after temporarily. "Not on the grounds of abuse, but on unsuitable housing."

"But – can't I take her?" Martha asked, defeated.

Turning to her, the magistrate said, "As soon as your housing situation has been sorted out, get your solicitor to bring you straight back to this court and we will remove the care order."

I naively thought it should only take a matter of a day or two, so that seemed like a good resolution. But if I had known what was about to happen I would have asked them not to grant a care order and I would have taken Sally to my parents' while we were waiting for Martha's housing situation to be resolved.

On leaving the court, our solicitor rushed off, probably to another appointment. Then, I spotted Sharon Daily in the near-distance, walking briskly away from the court, so I ran to catch up with her.

"How long will it be before you can find Martha somewhere to live so that she can have

Sally back?" I asked her.

"She won't be having her back," Daily told me.

This confused me. "But the magistrates have just said that Martha and Sally should be reunited when Martha gets suitable accommodation," I said.

"Silly old bags," Daily replied. "What do they know?"

It is hard to describe the emotions I felt in response to Daily's remark. The magistrates had all but disproved the allegations and yet the social workers were proceeding as if the magistrates were irrelevant! Daily was clearly annoyed at being subjected to the magistrate's searching questions and having her authority as a social worker challenged: something they were not used to, at that time. The social workers considered themselves not bound by the law, believing they could use court orders when it suited them and disregard them when it did not.

Social services had led us to believe that Sally had received very serious injuries and that Martha had even confessed to inflicting them. All this time, Martha had continually denied having hurt Sally. And as it turned out, Martha was apparently being truthful – unlike the social workers.

I immediately went to a phone box to call the solicitor, but he had not yet got back to his office; so I called back half an hour later. I finally spoke to the solicitor about the situation regarding Martha's housing and social services' response to the outcome of the court hearing.

I expected him to say he would take it back to court. Instead, he replied, "Well, they must know what they are doing. They will do what's in Sally's best interests, so we will have to go along with them."

After this event, Martha's already fragile mental state began to deteriorate rapidly, and on her visiting the doctor, he recommended that she see a psychiatrist. An appointment was made, and the psychiatrist recommended that Martha should attend a psychiatric hospital to be assessed. On **22 February 1986**, just seven days after the care order court case, Martha admitted herself into the psychiatric hospital voluntarily.

While she was in hospital, an appointment was made for Sally to be taken to visit her, and a few days later Sally was brought in by her foster mother, Jean, and a social worker. I was also present. I preferred to attend as many meetings involving social workers as possible, since by this time, I had become aware that they were masters of the art of distorting and misinterpreting what you said to them.

The meeting seemed to mainly focus on Martha's condition and the best way forward. The hospital psychiatrist asserted that the most appropriate measure would be to reunite Martha and Sally, in order to re-establish the bond between them.

The social worker said that the decision was up to Jean, the foster mother, as she knew what was best for the baby!

Jean said, "No, Martha is too dangerous."

I sat open-mouthed, while the psychiatrist again stated that he believed Martha posed no danger to Sally and to reunite them was a matter of urgency to allow the mother–baby bond to be re-established. These were the same words that the guardian ad litem had used at the court hearing.

"A mother and baby unit is available within the hospital," the psychiatrist told us. "Martha and Sally can be together under continuous specialist supervision in a stress-free environment. In my professional opinion, this would be the best therapy for Martha – and also, best for the baby."

Again, Jean disagreed.

The psychiatrist pointed out to Jean that, on many occasions, Martha had visited the child at the foster parents' home. During these visits, only Jean, Martha and the baby had been present.

"Martha is a much bigger and stronger woman than you," the psychiatrist continued, addressing Jean. "If you thought Martha was such a danger to the child, why would you allow her into your home where you would not be able to protect yourself, let alone the baby?"

Jean shrugged.

The psychiatrist again confirmed that the hospital had specialist staff on duty twenty-four hours a day in the mother and child unit and that Sally would be perfectly safe. But Jean was adamant that Sally would not be reunited with Martha.

The psychiatrist gave a heavy sigh and slapped his notes down on his desk. "If you are not prepared to follow my advice, there is nothing else I can do."

He clearly could not understand Jean's opposition to his recommendation.

Martha's stay in hospital served little purpose, which I feel was due to the psychiatrist's advice not being followed.

When I say "hospital", rather than this, it had the appearance of the "haunted house on the hill". It was one of those large Victorian buildings with staircases that were wide enough to park a double-decker bus sideways on them. I would not say that it was an extremely unpleasant place to visit, but it was definitely unsettling, although apparently there were a few laughs to be had. Martha once told me about a visit to the hospital shop she made. Not to buy anything specific – she went just for a walk and for something to do. On her way, she met up with a fellow patient, Sue.

"Are you off to the shop?" asked Sue. When Martha confirmed that she was, she advised, "Don't go the front way! If you do, you'll have to pay for stuff. Follow me."

Sue led Martha through parts of the building that she didn't know and as they came to a door, Sue said, "Sssshhhh. You have to be very quiet."

The door, as it turned out, led into the shop's storeroom at the back. Sue took several bags out from her clothing and began to fill them, saying to Martha, "Well, get what you want then!"

Martha had only gone with the intention of looking, or maybe buying one or two small things, and didn't have a bag with her. She felt uncomfortable with the idea of just taking something and not paying for it, but then something caught her eye and she just could not resist it. It was an enormous fresh cream gateau in the chiller cabinet. Now, bear in mind that in those days this type of cake was very expensive, unlike today, when you can buy them cheaply from supermarkets. Back then, it was normal to buy only a slice of this sort of cake. So, to have a whole large fresh cream gateau in front of you, calling to you to eat it – what else could you do, but oblige?

"We can't hang about," Sue had said, indicating that it was time to go, but Martha wouldn't leave without eating at least some of the cake.

Obviously, Martha could not take it back to her room because people would see it, so she decided to eat what she wanted while she was still in the storeroom.

"Have you ever tried to eat a gateau without a fork or spoon?" she asked me, when she was recounting this tale. "It's impossible to take a bite from it without getting it all over your face!"

She closed her eyes and buried her face in the cake, taking big mouthfuls of the creamy delight. When she pulled her face away, Sue screamed with laughter.

"Ah-ha-ha-ha!" she doubled over, barely able to speak. "State... state of you!"

Martha's face and hair were absolutely covered with cream and cake. Sue took a mirror out of her bag so that Martha could see herself. She looked as if she'd been hit squarely in the face in a cream-pie fight, and shrieked with laughter, herself.

They were now both laughing so loudly that the door from the shop opened and the horrified shopkeeper saw them and shouted, "What are you two doing in here?"

Sue gasped for breath in between guffaws, then merely said, "We're mental, so you can't do anything!"

And they walked out of the shop in fits of laughter.

"You don't seem mental," Martha said, after their giggles subsided.

"Neither do you," said Sue and she confessed that every few months or so, if she felt like a break from her husband and children she would go to her doctor complaining that life was getting on top of her and she needed a break because she could not take much more pressure.

Her doctor would then send her to the psychiatric hospital where, in Sue's words, "It's like being on holiday! You can do as you like, your food is cooked for you, there's no washing clothes or house cleaning! Then, after a week or two of taking it easy, I tell the doctor that I feel able to cope with life again – and they send me home."

It turned out that the woman was a regular patient at the hospital.

"But how does your husband cope while you're away?" Martha asked her.

"Oh, he comes visiting every evening, and brings a bag of dirty washing with him. I take it to the hospital laundry next day and have it washed."

"No!" said Martha, her eyes wide.

"Yeah. I give him the clean washing to take home on his next visit. Oh, and at meal times, I put hospital food into a separate bag for him to take home – for his and the kids' tea. So, you, know – we all win."

Martha would regale me with all of Sue's exploits and it made me laugh, just listening to it all. Talk about working the system!

Chapter 3

After Martha left the hospital, it was agreed by social workers and Jean that Martha was to be allowed to visit Sally at Jean's house during the day time.

It seemed that Jean's opposition to the doctor's recommendation in the hospital was merely to prevent mother and daughter from being reunited and not because Martha posed a threat. Why else was she being allowed to visit now, if she was considered so dangerous?

Martha visited Sally several times, but she said it was not going well. Martha had completely lost all confidence in her ability to be a mother.

"There's something wrong with me. Sally always seems to cry when I hold her."

At weekends, I started to go along with Martha, to visit, and I saw immediately what was happening.

We would go in, and Jean would thrust Sally into Martha's arms and, faced by unfamiliar smells and people, Sally would begin to cry immediately. Child and mother had been separated for weeks and weren't used to one another.

But Jean didn't offer Martha any help – no guidance like "hold her like this" or "gently rock her like this, until she feels comfortable with you".

Instead, when the baby cried, Jean would take Sally straight back, almost snatching her off Martha. All happening in about thirty seconds.

"See? This happens every time Martha holds her," Jean said, shaking her head in disapproval, trying to give the impression that Sally did not like her mother.

As soon as Sally was back in Jean's arms, she would produce a chocolate button from her pocket and put it in Sally's mouth, stopping her crying straight away.

A few minutes after the chocolate button had been eaten, Jean suddenly and unexpectedly pushed Sally into my arms, saying "Go to daddy".

Sally looked at me in horror and her lip trembled. I could see by her face that she was about to cry again. Now, I am from a big family and there always seemed to be babies in our house, brothers' babies or sisters' babies, and I liked to think I knew how to handle them.

Sally's bottom lip pouted and her mouth opened, but before the first sound of a cry left her mouth, I spun around, swinging her and lowering and raising her like on a merry-go-round, and I began making the strangest noises.

She had a look of shock on her face initially, but she was soon laughing and making baby noises. By the expression on Jean's face, it seemed as if it took her by surprise, too.

Martha grinned in relief and pleasure. But what happened next surprised me very much. Jean took the bag of chocolate buttons from her pocket and began rattling it in the air, trying to attract Sally's attention. She could see that I was interacting with Sally, and to me, her action was an attempt to stop it. She did not succeed. For the time we were there – about an hour – Sally was with me, laughing and cooing.

After we left the foster parents' house I asked Martha, "Does she always give Sally chocolate?"

"Yeah." Martha confirmed that she did.

I frowned, pondering on this. The more I thought about it, it reminded me of puppy-training, and how you offer training treats as rewards. It seemed to me that Sally was being trained to cry when she was in Martha's arms.

I can tell you that by now, Martha's mental state was not good.

She was withdrawn when I mentioned Sally and admitted that "I don't want to visit in the week She told me that because of the way Sally acted towards her, but would wait for the weekend and visit with me.

She told me how proud she had felt when I was holding Sally and making her laugh. Surely, Jean should have been trying to create this sort of interaction between Martha and Sally – and not trying to destroy the relationship between them, which to me seemed to be her intention.

The following Saturday we visited Sally and I was soon making her laugh, and there was no attempt by Jean to use chocolate to attract Sally's attention. After playing with her for about ten minutes, I said to Martha, "Here, it's your turn now."

Everything went quiet and Martha's eyes widened in shock. I put Sally in Martha's arms and saw the baby's bottom lip drop. I knew what was about to happen, but I was prepared: taking a packet of chocolate buttons from my pocket.

"It's OK, Martha. Dance about with her like I did," I told her, and popped a button into Sally's mouth while she was in Martha's arms. She was as happy as could be.

"David! I don't like Sally eating chocolate. It's not good for her!" Jean said, incredibly.

"I presumed the occasional one doesn't hurt." Before she could reply, I added, "If you prefer, I'll buy the same brand you give her."

"Well, I suppose the occasional one or two won't hurt her," she responded flatly.

A day or two later, I was at work when Martha phoned me, in tears.

She said she had just been to visit Sally and while she was there, Jean told her she was no good as a mother and that if she had any decency in her she would allow Sally to be adopted. Then she told Martha she was no longer welcome at the foster home and instructed her not to visit again.

"That's not right!" I cried. I could only advise Martha to do something as soon as possible, since I was helpless. They wouldn't listen to me. They reckoned I had no say in it at all, even though I was Sally's father. "Phone social services and tell them what's happened."

When Martha called social services and explained what had been said, she was told by a social worker, "Well, we can't force her to let you into her house. If you want to see Sally again, you'll have to make an appointment to meet at the social services office."

Martha was at a loss how to contest this, so she conceded. It was either that, or never see Sally again. Obviously, these visits would only occur at the convenience and under the supervision of Jean. Due to the fact that Jean would have to travel to the office, it was agreed that there could only be one visit per week.

I was desperate, but out of my depth. The injustice! I spoke to various members of my family about Martha not being allowed to visit the foster parents' house.

My sister-in-law, Ruth, who had originally called social services on our behalf, said, "I saw Jean in Bankham town centre, so I stopped to talk to her."

During the conversation Ruth told her, "It's such a shame. Tell you what, though... if the worst came to the worst, I'd adopt Sally, myself."

Jean sniffed and said, "No need. There's a list of people wanting to adopt her. And we're at the top of the list."

My blood ran cold. This was all making more sense, now. She wanted Sally for herself.

Martha saw Sally at the social services office and before leaving, made another appointment for the following week.

I received a phone call from the social worker and was told that the foster parents would allow *me* to visit Sally at their house, if I so wished. These visits could be early evenings, after I had finished work; but I would be only allowed to go alone – I had to be without Martha. My mind reeled with anger and suspicion, but I said I would do this.

On the afternoon of Martha's next appointment to see Sally, I received a phone call from Martha, crying.

"I got to the social services office," she sniffed, "But Sally wasn't there. And... and... the social worker said... that if I wanted to see Sally again, I'd have to sign a document." Here, she broke down.

The document, it transpired, was an authorisation to allow Sally to be adopted. My stomach rolled over with nausea and panic as I listened to Martha in between sobs. The social worker told her that if she did not sign the paper she would never see Sally again. But if she did, she would be allowed to see Sally just one last time – only to say goodbye to her.

"I said I would never sign it! I wouldn't give her away!"

Then the social worker told her they would just go to court and Martha's signature would not be needed. But Martha's consent now would make things easier for everyone – and allow her to see Sally one last time.

Martha left the social services office without signing the papers.

I told her, "Go and make an appointment with the solicitor. Tell them what they said!" Social services should not be allowed to act in this manner.

Martha saw the solicitor the following day, and he told her that social services appeared to be acting inappropriately. He said he would write a letter to them, stating that Martha must be allowed to see Sally.

Within a few days, Martha was told by social services that she would be allowed to see Sally again. But only once a week – and at the social services office.

I also received a phone call from social services, during which I was told that if *I* wanted to see Sally, I was welcome to visit the foster parents' home in the evening after I had finished work, but again, only on condition that Martha did not attend. I felt that something was going on, but I couldn't quite put my finger on it.

Around the same time, I received a phone call from Sharon Daily, the child protection worker, saying that she wanted to talk to me, and asking if she could come to my place of work. I agreed.

When we met, Daily told me, "I've come to the decision that Martha is never to be allowed to have Sally back."

"What?" I exclaimed. "Why?"

"Due to Martha's deteriorating mental state, it's considered too dangerous for Sally."

"But..."

Daily interrupted: "We're left with two options. The first, and most appropriate, action is for Sally to be adopted. But we need your signature and agreement that you will not oppose this action."

My heart leapt into my mouth. No way! And yet, suddenly, I had rights, as a father?

"The second option is for you to apply for custody of Sally."

My mind was whirling in blind panic. That was the better option, but it was impossible! I was running my own business, working all hours to get it off the ground. How could I look after a baby, single-handed? This option did not seem viable unless I gave up work to care for Sally full-time.

"I'll apply for custody, then," I said, anyway.

"Really?" she said sceptically. "How is that going to work, then?"

I told Daily that I would ask my older sister, Hilary, if she would care for Sally during the day. I would care for her in the evenings and weekends.

Daily did not seem very happy with this reply, but I pointed out that many working parents leave their children with child-minders during the day.

"Yes, but your sister is not a child minder," said Daily.

"Maybe not," I replied, "but she has A levels and O levels in English and Maths. She has two children of her own – both attending Grammar School."

Daily spent quite some time trying to talk me out of it, with reasoning such as, "Do you really want to spend a hard day at work and then have to go home and look after a baby in the evenings and at weekends?"

"I will do it."

And "What about when your friends go out for a drink and you're stuck at home?"

"My priority is Sally."

I was determined, and she couldn't talk me out of it.

The option I had chosen still depended on my sister agreeing to care for Sally, of course. Daily reluctantly said that if my sister agreed, then I would have to increase my contact time with Sally.

On my visits to see Sally at the foster parents' house, I was always made very welcome. I tended to Sally, feeding, bathing and putting her to bed. On Sundays, I would take her for a walk around the local park and on our return to the foster home, we would chat amicably and Jean would even invite me to share a late afternoon meal. I could not understand why they were so hostile towards Martha, yet so hospitable to me.

During one of my evening visits, Jean said that some time before, Martha had told her that she had chosen the name Sally, but I had chosen her middle name, Lucy.

Jean asked me, "Such a lovely name – Lucy. Would you prefer us to start calling her Lucy?"

I frowned, bewildered, and said no, seeing no reason to change, now.

It was then that Mike, the foster father, said, "Awww... we've always dreamt of having a baby girl – and if it ever happened, the name we've chosen is 'Lucia'. It's Norwegian for Lucy."

Jean gazed fondly at Sally, and added, "Isn't that a coincidence? Awww. It's a lovely name for a lovely little girl – Lucy."

"Right…" I said, with unease.

Chapter 4

A while later, a core group meeting was arranged at the foster parents' house. This meeting was to plan how to proceed with my application to get custody of Sally. The people present at this meeting were myself and Martha, the foster parents, a Bankham social worker, my sister, Hilary, and a male senior social worker who was based in Hemsgroute – a neighbouring town. The male social worker from Hemsgroute was to chair the meeting, and provide a more objective independent view.

The main topic of this meeting was the custody of Sally and the role of each person involved. During the meeting, the chair raised the point that his records showed that there appeared to have been no recent contact between mother and baby at the foster home, and he asked Martha if she no longer wished to see Sally.

Before Martha could answer, Jean said, "Oh, I had to stop Martha from visiting because my house was like Piccadilly station. I have to consider the welfare of my own children first."

The Bankham social worker then said, "Martha was told that she could visit Sally at Bankham social services office, but she has only done so on a few occasions."

It would appear that there was no mention in the Hemsgroute social worker's notes to indicate that Martha had been instructed to sign adoption papers and had been told by Bankham social workers that she could never see Sally again!

Nor was it recorded that visiting had only recently been restored after Bankham social services received our solicitor's letter insisting that they allow Martha to see her child.

The Hemsgroute social worker said, "I'm very concerned about Martha's limited amount of access and the obligation for her to see Sally at Bankham social services office. In my opinion, it isn't a very normal environment for a mother to visit her baby in."

During the meeting it had been mentioned that I had Sally for the whole day on Sundays. The Hemsgroute social worker suggested that to address Martha's limited access to her child, she should accompany me on a Sunday, as this would allow her access for a complete day.

"This must be better than the current

situation."

Jean said, "No. I disagree. This is "quality time" between Sally and Dave. It mustn't be spoilt by Martha being there."

The Bankham social worker agreed with Jean.

The Hemsgroute social worker had a confused look on his face and said, "From this meeting, I'm getting a strong feeling that a great amount of effort is being put into bringing David and Sally together. And yet, a similar amount of effort is being used to keep Martha and Sally apart."

"No, Jean and myself know the case," the Bankham social worker responded. "And we know what is best for the child."

Still, the outcome of the meeting was that I would apply for custody of Sally and, when granted, my sister Hilary would care for Sally during the daytime. Then, contrary to Jean and the Banham social worker's misgivings, myself and Martha would care for Sally in the evenings and at weekends.

The Hemsgroute social worker said, "The sooner David gets custody, the better. This will allow much more contact between mother and daughter."

I think it was about two or three days after this meeting that I was again visited at my place of work by Sharon Daily.

Daily told me, "We've changed our minds about the arrangements agreed at the previous meeting."

"What?" I couldn't understand.

"For us in Bankham Social Services to support your custody application, you must sever all ties with Martha and agree not to allow any contact between Martha and Sally."

I shook my head in disbelief. How could they just do that, out of the blue, after what had been agreed?

"Why are you *so* determined to break off any contact between Martha and Sally?" I asked her.

But all she said was, "It is our decision and if you do not agree to it then Bankham social services will have no option but to oppose your application for custody. And we will apply to the court for an adoption order."

My blood ran cold. There was no way I wanted that to happen, and I needed this to go smoothly to make sure Sally stayed with us – or at least, with me, in the first instance – until I could get advice and sort this out. Given this ultimatum, I had to agree to their terms, but I had begun to get the feeling that I was somehow being set up to take a fall and that Bankham social services were positioning themselves to step in, when I did.

"OK. I agree. No contact with Martha," I said, against all my instincts.

Daily's lips tightened. "However, before you can go any further, you will have to find suitable accommodation for yourself and Sally."

This struck in the heart. This was new, and that requirement hadn't been factored into my plans. At this time, I was living at my parents' house in Norisway, which saved me some costs while I was setting up my business, and having the family around would have helped. Admittedly, they didn't have a spare bedroom – but Sally was only a baby. My mind froze with the impossibility of setting all this up. It was overwhelming.

Daily told me that as soon as I had accommodation of my own, I would be able to have Sally come and stay with me on the occasional evening, and that this could gradually increase up to the time that I received custody.

I took this in, numbly. It all seemed vague, distant, dependent on so many things – and, in that moment, impossible. But I was willing to jump through whatever hoops were necessary, just to get custody. Just to stop them taking Sally from us, forever. I would have to play along and dance to their tune.

Before Daily left I asked her, "What about Martha? What help is there for her, considering her mental state is getting worse, with all this?"

"There is none," Daily replied. "Nothing can be offered to Martha. She will either come through it herself or she'll self-destruct."

And she turned her back and left. I could not believe that someone working in the social care sector was capable of such a cold-hearted response.

I told Martha what Sharon Daily had said, that she was not to have contact with me and Sally in order for me to be granted the custody order. It was not a very pleasant thing to have to say, but I had to comply with Bankham social services' requirements.

In despair, Martha left Bankham and moved into a bedsit in Birmingham. I was living in Norisway, Hambleshire, so I applied to Bradford Common council for housing. I explained the situation to the housing officer – that my daughter was in the care of Bankham social services and that as soon as I had suitable accommodation, the process of having Sally back could begin. The housing officer said that because of my circumstances I would be given priority status on the housing list and the next suitable property would be offered to me.

It all seemed to be looking good. The housing situation at that time was not as severe as it is today, so after having not heard anything for about a month, I thought I would give the housing department a call. I was told that nothing suitable had become available. Given that I had said on my application form that Norisway or any of the surrounding areas would be acceptable, and the fact I had been told that I was a priority case, their reply seemed a little strange. One person and a baby, happy to live anywhere? It wasn't as if I was a family of eight.

I waited another few weeks without hearing anything; then I called them again. The reply was the same: "Nothing available yet." I called the housing department every two weeks for approximately six months and always received the same reply: "nothing available".

Bankham social services were now voicing

their concerns that I was not making progress in finding accommodation and if I was not willing or able to find suitable accommodation in the not-too-distant future then Sally would have to be put up for adoption.

"I've tried everything!" I said, growing desperate. "What more can I do?"

A day or two after this warning from social services, I was at the foster parents' house, looking after Sally. At about seven o'clock in the evening, there was a knock at the door and when Jean opened it, it appeared that two social workers had decided to visit. I thought it was a strange time for them to be calling. It also seemed that Jean had been expecting them. As soon as the social workers sat down, Jean told me to take Sally upstairs for a bath and wash her hair.

She paused and then said, "Make sure you wash it properly, because I *will* check it!" She spoke to me like a child – almost implying that on previous occasions I had not done it properly.

Now, whenever Sally had her hair washed, whether by me or Jean, Sally would scream hysterically. Jean would always say, "When it's time for Sally to have her hair washed, then it must be washed – whether she screams and cries or not. If

Sally knows she can get out of having her hair washed by crying, you'll never get her to wash her hair."

I became convinced that this was an attempt to set me up, because I knew what was expected to happen: two social workers present, me bathing Sally – Sally begins screaming hysterically, foster mother runs upstairs like a superhero, to save the day. So, I took Sally for her bath and decided that if Jean wanted to see Sally's hair washed, then that is what she would see. I bathed Sally, but instead of pouring water over her head as usual, I just wet my hands and rubbed Sally's head as if I were playing with her. She chuckled. I did this several times, until her hair was totally wet and had actually been washed, without so much as a murmur. Jean shouted upstairs several times to check whether everything was alright, and I replied that yes, everything was fine.

After I had bathed Sally I took her downstairs and there were distinct looks of bewilderment from them all. I had wrapped Sally in a large towel, which also covered her head. The first thing Jean said was, "I told you to wash her hair."

I said, "I have washed her hair!"

Jean immediately snatched the towel from

Sally's head, expecting to see dry hair, and seeing it all wet and clean, her horrified face spoke volumes. She obviously couldn't ask why Sally hadn't screamed; but the hard set of her jaw showed me that her plan had been scuppered.

An intended disaster was definitely averted.

My sister Hilary, who had agreed to care for Sally during working hours, told me about someone she knew who lived in a flat not far from her house in Allbank. This person had arranged a new job in a different county and was therefore about to relinquish her tenancy. I phoned the housing department straight away and told them that this flat would soon be vacant and asked whether it would be possible for me to have the tenancy. The housing officer said that they could not allocate the property until it had become vacant but they would contact me when it was, and until that time I must wait – again.

After Hilary confirmed that the person had left the flat, I waited two weeks. Having heard nothing from the housing department, I decided to phone them. The housing officer said she could not tell me anything, other than the property had already been allocated.

"Has it been allocated to me?" I asked her, and she replied "No."

"But I'm a priority case!" I explained to her. "I've been waiting six months for housing, and I was the one who informed you about this property becoming vacant!"

She sounded genuinely concerned by what I had told her and said she would pass me over to a more senior housing officer who should be able to help me.

Another woman came to the phone and asked me in a very stern, abrupt and sarcastic manner, "Why do you think you are special enough to be a priority case? There are many more people out there far more deserving of accommodation than you."

My head buzzed with tension, but I remained polite. These people had to help me, so I knew it was no good getting angry.

I explained the situation with Sally to her and said, "Six months ago, I was told that I had a priority position on the housing list."

"Well, whoever told you that had no right. I can confirm that you're not even being considered for housing!"

"Why?" I gasped in shock. This made no

sense.

"You're not homeless. Your child is with foster parents – and has housing. You're living with your parents in Norisway, so you also have housing. Therefore, you're not a priority."

"I'm seeking custody of Sally," I explained. "But Bankham social services will only support my application if I have suitable housing to live in with her."

"If you get custody of your child and you are having to live apart, then we would consider you for housing," the housing officer then said. "But not until you get custody."

"But I've just told you I can't get custody until I get housing first!" I was so exasperated, I raised my voice. "And now you are saying I can't get housing until I have custody? How is that ever going to happen?"

"That's your problem to sort out," she said. "Don't bother calling us again until you have custody of your child."

Within minutes of putting the phone down on Bradford Common housing department, I called the solicitor to make an appointment, because as far as I was concerned, the housing department was putting me in a Catch-22 situation to avoid giving me housing.

When I met the solicitor, I explained what had been said between me and the housing department, and the solicitor said that the housing department were totally wrong. "If the lack of suitable housing is the only obstacle preventing a child currently in local authority care from returning to a natural parent, then the local authority has a legal duty to allocate suitable housing." He told me he would write a letter to them immediately, reminding them of their legal responsibility.

Within fourteen days of the solicitor sending the letter, I received a written offer of a flat in Allbank. Before I replied to the offer I went to have a look at the property, and it so happened that I knew the person who lived next door.

I knocked on his door to tell him that I had been offered the flat next to his.

His face screwed up and he said, "You're not seriously thinking of moving in there, are you? You must be mad."

"What's wrong with the place? You live in the next flat."

"Just thinking about it makes me itch," he said. "When the council moved the previous tenant out and the decorators were sent in to clean and decorate, they came running out shouting and screaming that the place was alive with fleas!"

I pulled a face, but he went on. "The fumigators were called in and said the place was so bad, they'd have to come back a few days later and fumigate it all again, just to be on the safe side!"

"Okay..." I blinked.

"After the fumigators gave the all-clear," he went on, "the cleaners and decorators came back. The cleaners said they'd never seen so many dead fleas!" I swallowed hard. "There were so many, they had to be swept up and filled a bucket!"

"Must be OK, now, though," I mumbled.

"And the decorators claimed it was almost impossible to paint the walls because they were thick with grease – as if they'd been soaked in something like old fat. It seemed to them that when the previous tenant wanted to change the chip pan oil, they'd simply thrown the old, dirty oil up the walls."

Hmmm. Beggars can't be choosers, I thought, so I went and got the key to have a look around. I was getting desperate. I also had the feeling in the back of my mind that, given the slightest opportunity, the social workers would turn on me – and taking too long to find somewhere to live might be just the excuse they needed. *Anyway, I thought, the flat can't be in too bad a state or the council couldn't let it.*

When I went inside, I actually liked the flat, but I could see what my friend meant about the walls. They had been painted in the standard council green colour, which isn't a bad colour in itself, but this green had become discoloured. It looked like the plaster had been soaked all over in dirty brown oil that seemed to be coming through the paint. It was not a pretty sight, but I thought to myself that wallpaper would solve the problem, so I decided to accept the flat and moved in.

For some reason, I didn't even give it a thought that if paint would not cover the oil, wallpaper paste was probably not going to stick to it either. I tried and I tried, but the paper wouldn't stick, so, as a short-term measure, I used drawing pins to hold the paper in place.

I was grateful for one thing, though: the fumigators had done a good job because I never saw a single flea in the place.

But I didn't know what to do about the wallpaper. Usually, when you put paste on wallpaper, the paste soaks into the paper and because the paste is clear, when it dries you cannot see it. My problem was that I was pasting over dirty oil, so the paste would become a horrible brown colour, and when it soaked into the paper and dried, the wallpaper had big brown stains all over it. I needed to get the place looking decent to get custody of Sally.

On one evening visit to see Sally at the foster parents' house, I happened to mention the problem I was having with the wallpaper not sticking to the walls and Mike, the foster father, said "I've done quite a lot of house decorating. I'll come and help you."

When he saw the state of the walls he told me, "You'll never get paper to stick to the walls unless you get the oil or grease out of the plaster!"

"How?"

He told me about a solvent I should get. "You'll need to keep painting it onto the walls until it kind of kills the oil enough for paper to stick."

So that's what I did. I painted the walls every evening for about two weeks and it did the trick. I dread to think how much old cooking oil had been thrown at those walls, and why.

The flat was now furnished and fit to live in, and social services said I could have Sally to stay overnight once a week, returning her to the foster home the following morning. Social services said we must do this once a week for a month or so, and if all went well, then we could increase Sally's stays with me to two evenings a week – and so on. It had been a long journey, against the odds, but it seemed as if my patience and hard work to meet all their requirements was paying off. In all this time, Martha and I were in touch, even though she had moved away. Her sadness and despair were obvious, and every time she rang, it was in the mild hope of some movement towards Sally coming home again. I couldn't offer her any guarantees – but I remained optimistic. It was all I had to cling onto.

On one of the evenings that Sally was not with me, I invited my friend from next door round for a drink to show him what an expert decorator I was. He complimented me on what a good job I had made of the place, and I explained all the technical problems involved when dealing with the oil slicks in the walls. It must have slipped my mind to mention that I had help with the decorating...!

"They killed all the fleas as well, then?" he said. "Because I haven't seen one."

I said, "No, there were a few tough buggers left that the fumigators couldn't kill, but I said to them, 'If you stay here, the only thing you'll get to eat is old cooking oil,' so they upped and left. I think they moved next door to yours!"

He tutted and punched me on the arm.

Chapter 5

In **September 1988** I applied for custody of Sally at Bradford Common Magistrates Court, but I was told by the court that there was still a care order in place on Sally from a Bankham court – and that until this order had been removed, I could not proceed with my application for custody. This was ridiculous! Why was I allowed to go to court if this was going to happen?

I had to explain the situation to Bankham social services. But they must have known I could not get custody in a Hambleshire court while there was still a care order in force from a court in their area.

It seemed that the Bankham social workers were attempting to give the impression that they were trying to help me, but in reality, I was getting no help from them at all. It felt as if I was up against acts of passive resistance. I was having to take every step forward without any real useful advice.

It is important to realise that it can take many months to get before a court and if for some reason the court cannot proceed, then it can take many months to get back there again. By this time, Sally had been in care for four years, which was virtually all her life. It felt like a large chunk of mine, too. But I would never give up.

I had a phone call from Bankham social services asking if they could come and visit the flat I was intending to take Sally to live in. The social worker arrived and we had a good long talk. She told me that she liked the flat and would have no objection to Sally living there. We also talked about various things that were happening at the time. One of the topics we talked about was a news story about social workers taking a large number of children from a small town in Scotland. It was said that a large number of the children had been removed due to alleged child abuse.

"How could so many children in one small town *all* have been abused by their parents?" I asked the social worker.

She replied, "Actually, a study has shown that approximately one child in three are being abused by a family member or a close family friend."

"That can't be right!" I queried her claim, but she insisted it was correct.

The social workers I'd seen on the news had

said that they could see if a child was being abused by how it acted, with such indicators as a child wanting to sit on a grown-up's lap or holding onto their leg. I asked the social worker how there could be anything wrong in that, pointing out that Sally would sit on my lap and sometimes hold onto my leg.

"Would you call that abuse?" I asked.

She said, "No, because we know you, so for your daughter to sit on your lap, it's perfectly normal."

This seemed to me a very strange attitude: you could have two adults interacting with children in exactly the same way, and one adult could be accused of abuse but the other adult would not, purely on the basis that a social worker could say "we know that person would not abuse the child".

It seemed that in accusations of abuse, it depended on whether the social worker decided to interpret the actions of the adult as signs of abuse or as normal interaction, based on how the social worker views or has been told how to view the adult. In other words, if they like you, your actions are normal; if the social worker does not like you, your actions are interpreted as abuse. Several years later, this theory would play out, as social workers went from supposedly supporting me to openly opposing me because they said I "collude to deceive professionals" and "distort facts".

Soon, Bankham social services went to court and had the care order removed, allowing Bankham court to give me guardianship of Sally! Now, it seemed, if social services needed to get to court, they could do so in a matter of days. Why didn't they allow me to apply for custody while they were in court instead of only guardianship? This just meant I would have to make yet another court appointment.

My solicitor applied for another court date in Bradford Common, and luckily, we didn't have to wait long. The court date was set for **24 September 1988**. Within a few minutes of being in court, the court clerk announced that there was a problem: there was no evidence to show that I was Sally's natural father!

He asked if Sally's mother was in the court and my solicitor said no. The clerk said that only the natural parent of a child could be given custody and without sufficient evidence that I was indeed Sally's natural father the application for custody could not proceed!

"Not again," I thought to myself.

My solicitor's only reply to the court clerk was, "But there is no evidence to show that Mr Jordan is *not* Sally's natural father."

Even I thought 'what a stupid reply that was' and I remember wondering if my solicitor actually knew anything.

I think the court clerk was a bit bewildered by that reply, too. He said, "I cannot accept that as a valid argument."

The court clerk said, "Your only option would be to contact the child's mother and either bring her to court, or get a statement from her confirming that you are the child's natural father."

My heart stopped, but I felt a tap on my shoulder. I looked around and there was a woman seated just behind me who introduced Herself, saying, "I represent Bradford Common probation service. I've been asked to follow up your case." She said, "I'm a retired barrister. Would you allow me to address the court on your behalf?"

Desperate for any assistance, I immediately said yes, and she then asked my solicitor if he objected.

He said, "If you could assist in any way, I would be grateful."

This woman addressed the court and said,

"Bankham social services have applied to Bankham court to have the care order removed, and for Mr Jordan to be given guardianship until such time as he can apply for custody of Sally." She paused for breath, then went on: "This would suggest that Bankham social services and Bankham court have sufficient grounds to be satisfied that Mr Jordan is the child's natural parent – since only a natural parent can apply for custody of a child."

The magistrates began talking with the court clerk.

The woman warned me, "In a few moments, you'll be asked to make an affidavit (a statement on oath)."

My bewildered look allowed her to explain. She said I would be asked some personal questions about whether I had a sexual relationship with the child's mother at the time of the child's conception and if, to the best of my knowledge, the mother of the child was not having a relationship with anyone else at that time.

"Right. OK," I said. I was certain of my ground, there.

She also asked me if I was aware of what was in Bankham social services' files concerning this case. I told her I was not.

She said, "I've read the case files and I was horrified that such a straightforward case could have been handled in such a way, and over such a long period of time, that it has all but destroyed the family unit."

She said it seemed that the child's mother may have had some problems and might need some help, but she could find nothing in the files that should have led Bankham social services to have vilified Martha in such a way.

I could hardly believe it. She was a godsend!

She said that she knew some people in Bankham local authority and would try to find out what had gone wrong in this case. I could feel myself getting excited with hope.

I was then asked to stand and make a statement to the court and was asked the very questions that the woman had mentioned. She certainly knew the law. My solicitor remained silent as this woman took over the role of representing me, and I thank God she did. There was simply no comparison between the abilities of my solicitor and this woman's.

While the magistrates were discussing the details, the woman asked me if I had any objections to the child's mother having access to the child and I told her that I did not. "In fact, I've always wanted it. It's not right that they've stopped Martha from seeing her."

They announced that they were granting me custody!

As soon as the court said they would grant custody of Sally to me, the woman asked them if the order could allow for access by the mother and for it to be shown on the custody order.

Custody was duly granted to me and the custody order stated that Martha was to have access to Sally!

The ex-barrister told me that she had done this to hopefully allow the child's mother to have a part in her life. She instructed me to make sure I kept a copy of the custody order, because she had the feeling that at some time in the future, I might need it.

I heard no more from the probation services worker after that. I was only too happy with the outcome. And I decided not to enquire if she had found anything wrong about the way Bankham social services had conducted the case, for fear of reprisals.

And fear of reprisals I certainly had. Social services had made it clear from Day One that they wanted all ties between Martha and Sally to be broken. Why else would they disregard the court's wishes at the first care order hearing? Referring to the magistrates as "silly old women", then going against the psychiatrist's advice to reunite Martha and Sally in the mother and child unit at the psychiatric hospital, and why did they offer to support my application for custody on the condition that I did not allow any contact between Martha and Sally? We now had this ex-barrister at the custody hearing, telling me that Bankham social services had dealt with the situation in a totally inappropriate way, that their actions had all but destroyed the family unit and that Martha's name should be put on the custody order, allowing her access to Sally.

What would Bankham social services' response be, if they found out that the court had given Martha access? I didn't want to stir the waters. It is important to realise the powers that social workers have, since it appears that they can disregard court orders and medical advice if the order or advice is not to their liking.

They are a very powerful body of people, but it would not be until a couple of years later, after we had moved back to Bankham, that we would experience the full, furious reprisals of Bankham social services.

Martha contacted me about a week after the hearing and I told her that not only had I been awarded custody of Sally, but that the custody order stated that she could have access! So, the very next day, she came to visit. It was almost heartbreaking to see how shy she was, first of all, on seeing Sally after so long. But her love was obvious, and with my encouragement and support, they started to forge a relationship again. And we tentatively started to believe that things were better. She began to visit regularly, with increasing pleasure and comfort, and about a month after the custody hearing, it only made sense that Martha moved in with Sally and me. We could start to be a proper family at last!

We were happy – almost deliriously happy at times, although I was aware that it was a big adjustment for us all. However, it soon became apparent that Martha's mental state had suffered badly. Over the intervening years, her condition had become progressively worse. She wasn't just depressed and anxious – she would often accuse neighbours of plotting against her and she became very suspicious of everything and everybody. There was an extent to which, I couldn't blame her. She'd basically been called an unfit mother, and had her child taken off her for years. She hardly knew who she could trust. But her suspicions of the neighbours seemed unnecessarily extreme and bordering on the irrational. This resulted in us having to move house many times. Although we tried to run away from the neighbours, the problem followed us, and I was worried about Martha's mental state. She wasn't a danger to anyone, but was clearly in need of some help.

We were still living in Allbank, Hambleshire, when, on one of Martha's bad days, I decided to phone Hambleshire social services and ask what advice they could give me in pursuing help for Martha. A male social worker was put on the phone to talk to me. He asked me what the problems were, and I explained how Martha was acting towards neighbours.

He asked, "Is Martha violent towards Sally?"

"No. No way. Not at all!"

An odd question then followed: "Do her actions upset her? Martha, that is? Is she upset by what she does?"

I said they were not, thinking what a silly thing it was to ask. But he then asked whether

Martha's actions were upsetting me, to which I replied, "Yes, of course they are!"

Then, came what I call social workers' twisted logic: "If Martha's actions are not bothering her, but they are bothering you – then how I see it, it's you that needs the help and not Martha."

I said in a sarcastic manner, "And what about the neighbours? Do you think they need help, too?"

"We cannot give help to your neighbours, but if you would like to make an appointment to come and see us, I am sure we could help you to handle the stresses that you are feeling," he replied.

My reply to him was completely out of character for me, as I snapped, "You stupid idiot!" and slammed the phone down.

I felt as if I was talking to a brick wall.

After various house exchanges, we finally moved back to Bankham, taking a house in Primmers Lane, the same street in which Martha was living when all the problems with social services started.

During our time back at Primmers Lane, our family grew: Rachel was born in **February 1991** and John was born **March 1992**.

Early in 1995, Martha and I went to see Dr Carter, our GP, about Martha's problems. The doctor said she could refer Martha to a psychiatrist. Initially, Martha said no, but after a little persuasion, she agreed.

In **April 1995,** Martha was diagnosed as suffering from severe paranoid psychosis and possible schizophrenia. I asked Dr Kite, the consultant psychiatrist, why the report said "possible schizophrenia" and he explained that for a clinical diagnosis of schizophrenia, a person needs to display a certain number of symptoms, of which Martha was displaying all but one – the symptom of hearing voices. The doctor noted that she appeared to hear noises, not voices, and she assumed these noises to be neighbours causing disturbance, for the purpose of annoying her. He felt that she seemed to have a variation of schizophrenia.

Then, thinking of our children, I asked Dr Kite if Martha's condition was hereditary. To my relief, he said no.

He said that Martha's illness seemed to occur spontaneously, "But it is thought by many mental health professionals that it can be brought on in some people by stress or a very traumatic incident in their lives."

That made sense to me. I wonder how stressful it is for a woman to have her baby pulled out of her arms in the street without any warning? Then to be wrongly accused of violence, and not allowed to see her child for years? If that isn't traumatic, I don't know what is.

In **July 1995,** we were contacted by Bankham social services. They said they had reason for concern because the health visitor had reported difficulty in gaining access to John. She said that on previous visits, in her opinion, John was not voicing enough clear words for a child his age (three, at the time).

I told the social worker, "Martha's only missed two appointments with the health visitor. So it's not a case of Martha never taking John, or trying to avoid the health visitor – it was just two missed visits, that's all."

The social worker said that because the health visitor had not seen John recently and because of the health visitors concerns about John's language ability, they wanted to visit the house.

"OK, come then," I said, puzzled. I was sure they would find nothing amiss.

Two social workers arrived at the house on the first visit. One of these was a child protection worker called Kathleen Archer. I did not think at the time, but why should a child protection worker be one of the first to visit – just because of two missed appointments with the health visitor?

They stayed for about thirty minutes. In that time, Kathleen Archer spoke to the children, but not as if they were children – she spoke to them as if they were adults. "Right, children, I'm wondering if you can explain to me what the circumstances are, regarding your home situation?"

So, all three were a little reluctant to talk. I don't think it helped matters that Archer was dressed as you would normally expect a man to dress – in a suit and waistcoat, complete with a tie. And she also had a man's very short style of hair. I think this totally confused the children. In fact, Archer's appearance was commented on by my solicitor at a court meeting, some time later.

At the end of their visit, Kathleen Archer said that she had got very little response from Rachel and John when she tried to interact with them and she considered all three children to be severely developmentally delayed.

I totally disagreed with her; I felt that the children were of normal ability for their ages. They had just been told not to speak to strangers. And to them, there were very few people stranger than Kathleen Archer.

Archer said that because of her concerns for the development of the children, she was going to arrange for a child protection conference to be held on **1 August 1995**.

"Oh, come on!" I told her, "You're exaggerating and completely overreacting!"

She replied, "With all the physical injuries Sally suffered as a baby and the fact that you allowed access between Martha and Sally when social services had expressly forbidden it, we had no option but to investigate your family. It's a good thing that we have done – because of the poor development of all three children."

My blood ran cold. I realised, then, why they had come calling again.

I tried to explain to her the outcome of the first full care order meeting. I told her what the magistrates had said and, "As far as me allowing Martha access to see Sally – it was Bradford Common court that had allowed this, so I was only abiding by the conditions on the custody order!"

"You are distorting the details of past events," Archer insisted and she wanted to hear none of it.

I pointed out, "You've been at the house for approximately thirty minutes! How on earth could you make such an assessment in that time?"

I also questioned why the schools had not mentioned anything to us, if the children were as bad as she was describing them.

Kathleen Archer claimed that John's speech was severely delayed for a child of his age and that she wanted him to see a specialist, which I felt was ridiculous – and for a three-year-old, he was completely normal.

I could tell by her tone of voice and body language that she had set the course of her intended actions even before she had entered the house. I feel that they had wanted to take action against us, but they'd had to wait for an opportunity. The non-attendance at John's two health visitor meetings and the fact that Martha had now been formally diagnosed as suffering from a mental health condition gave them that opportunity.

The day after Kathleen Archer's visit to our house, I made an appointment to see the doctor. I told the doctor of Archer's opinion about John's speech level and asked if she could arrange for John to be assessed by a speech and language specialist.

The doctor said, "If John is talking and you

can understand him... and he can understand you –
then it seems strange that social services should be
concerned. After all, he's only three years old."

But because it was social services voicing
concerns, the doctor agreed to arrange for both
Rachel and John to see a specialist for assessment.

We took Rachel and John to see the speech
and language therapist, and after the first
assessment, we were told that both Rachel and
John were actually advanced for their ages.
However, the speech therapist said that because
social services had voiced concerns, then it would
be best if a course of appointments were made for
the children to see the specialist – even though
they did not need them. The speech therapist said
this should keep social services happy.

What I did not tell the doctor or the speech
therapist was that I had not informed social
services at this stage that the children were being
assessed or of the outcome of the assessment. I
viewed the social workers (child protection team)
with distrust and suspicion. Kathleen Archer had
wanted to take the children to be assessed and I
had refused, saying there was nothing wrong with
them.

I remain convinced that if social services had

arranged for the children to be assessed by their own specialist, the results would have shown them to be below normal development.

It is important to realise that if a child is shown to be developmentally delayed – and that this is due to poor parenting, then this constitutes abuse and the children can be removed from the home. As I was later told by Kathleen Archer, removal of the children is the only option in this case. I had one hell of a fight on my hands.

It seems too much of a coincidence that Martha was diagnosed with a mental health condition in April 1995 and social services turned up in July 1995, supposedly based on two missed appointments with the health visitor. Now, there was to be a child protection conference on **1 August 1995**.

Chapter 6

Martha and I attended the child protection conference and at the meeting, without any forewarning, we were told that Sally's school were now saying that they had serious concerns about Sally and about the many times she'd had to see the school nurse. The school's headmistress, Mrs Phillips, and another woman, the school secretary, I believe, were there. Mrs Bell, Sally's last class teacher, was not at the meeting.

As the meeting was taking place in August, this meant that Sally had now finished at Oldenhurst First School and was waiting to start at Hillsway Middle School. The woman that I took to be the secretary from Oldenhurst First School was trying to paint a grim picture of Sally at school. She said that she had asked for the school medical report to be delivered so that she could demonstrate the school's serious concerns, but the report had not yet arrived.

She was clearly agitated and asked several times, "Where is the report? It should have been here by now."

Suddenly, there was a knock on the door and

the woman got up and ran to it. She actually ran! It was, indeed, the medical report, and on her way back to her seat, she held it above her head, waving it and saying, "This is the report!"

She was grinning like a Cheshire cat and it was clear that all the other people present were just as eager as she was to hear this report.

As she began to look at it, turning through several pages, the expression on her face dropped. She mumbled a few noises, then almost reluctantly and quietly said, "It seems that all Sally's appointments with the school nurse have been about her eyes and the need to get eye glasses..." before raising her voice and continuing with, "but this does show a general trend."

At the meeting, a lot had been said about Sally's previous injuries and I think the attendees were expecting the nurse's report to contain reference to physical abuse. However, I repeated what I had previously told Kathleen Archer, the child protection worker: that the alleged injuries that Sally had suffered as a baby had been dismissed by the magistrates as having not been possible.

These people let you talk and then dismiss what you tell them because it is not what they want to hear. Regardless of all evidence to the contrary – all three children were put on the at-risk register! Social services decided they wanted Martha, Rachel and John to attend a local children's charity family centre one day a week. They told us that Sally was not required to go, since she was in full time education. We were told it was for the purpose of assessing Martha's parenting skills. I said that as I would be taking them all in the car, that I would also attend.

I am glad I did, because somebody had to witness this, and Martha was in no fit state to stand up for herself.

On our first visit to this family centre, we were told by Linda Berry, one of the family centre staff, that the staff there were completely impartial and would make an unbiased assessment of the family. We were shown a copy of the social services referral form, which stated that Martha was a paranoid schizophrenic. I asked them to alter this, as Martha had been diagnosed as *possibly* suffering from schizophrenia. According to the referral, there had also been violence between Martha and myself in front of the children and violence involving the children.

"What?" I gasped. "But that isn't true at all!"

As if to cover this eventuality, the referral also stated that I minimised any concerns, distorted facts and colluded to deceive professionals.

I refuted all the allegations, of course, but this probably just affirmed social services claims. Again, I was in some kind of nightmare Catch-22 situation.

I asked Linda Berry, "How can you possibly make an impartial assessment of the family, when the referral is so distorted? And the details include lies!"

Berry said that they were professionals and qualified to make impartial assessments.

I totally disagreed with this. "Your ability to be impartial has been compromised by that damning report! The very fact the referral form says I distort facts and collude to deceive professionals makes it impossible for you to carry out a fair and impartial assessment!" I cried, in exasperation. "Any observations you make will be influenced by that false referral form! You can't be objective! That isn't fair!"

I could tell by Berry's facial expression that my comments had not gone down well with her. I would soon find out exactly how impartial they were.

At the end of our first visit to this family centre, Linda Berry said, "I have concerns about John's speech ability. I consider him delayed for his age."

I frowned. I was keeping the assessment we'd had done up my sleeve, because I wanted to know what she had to say. Martha sat quietly worried, her eyes haunted by past experience.

Berry said, "I understand from child protection worker, Kathleen Archer, that you will not allow John to go for speech therapy."

"He doesn't need it."

"And that you're in denial about John's problems."

I rolled my eyes skywards. How could I win? If I denied anything, I proved them right.

"This gives me serious cause for concern," she went on.

What a coincidence, I thought. She was told by social services that John was delayed in his speech and that I refused to allow him to go to speech therapy, and now Berry was parroting back exactly the same things as social services. What happened to her ability to be impartial?

I asked Berry, "Are you a qualified speech and language specialist?"

"No," she said she was not, "but I am a professional child worker and that is qualification enough. So, I have no choice but to…"

"As it happens, John and Rachel have, in fact, been sent by our doctor to be assessed by a professional speech and language therapist," I decided to tell her, "and this expert in the field has said that both children are actually advanced for their ages."

Berry's eyes widened in surprise. "I was told you'd refused to allow John to be assessed."

"I simply refused to allow Kathleen Archer to arrange it. I asked my GP."

"Well, I disagree with whoever assessed John," she said bitterly. "In my opinion, he is delayed."

"But the real expert says the opposite," I reiterated.

Berry then said, "Well, I also feel that John is showing signs of severe behavioural problems."

"What?" I didn't know what they were going to come up with next! Martha sat with her fingernails in her mouth, her sad eyes hinting at the fear she felt. I knew she was anticipating the worst.

Berry explained, "In my view, he doesn't know how to play appropriately."

"What do you mean?"

"He wants to spend the whole time playing with toy cars in the play area..."

"He's a three-year-old boy, for Christ's sake!" I cried. "What do you expect him to do? Recite Shakespeare?"

I could see that Berry was not pleased with my comments. She then claimed that John seemed quiet and withdrawn when we had first arrived in the morning, but had livened up in the afternoon.

"We're very concerned about this," she warned. "We don't know the reason for it."

I began to believe that there was something sinister going on. The speech and language therapist had told us the children were advanced, yet these other so-called professionals were now saying that they were delayed, due to bad parenting! I believe that the local family centre staff were working under social services' instructions, coming to assessment conclusions as directed by social services. I also believe the staff genuinely thought that they were dealing with a person who was out to deceive them and who distorted facts, as the referral form had intimated. There was no way they could take me seriously after that damning indictment!

By telling Linda Berry that I believed the content of the referral form meant the staff's ability to make an impartial assessment of us had been compromised, I was doing the one thing you should never do to a social worker, whether they work for a national charity or the local authority: I was challenging their views and their professional competence.

But what other option did I have? It had become clear that the staff were not only unwilling or unable to be impartial but were showing every sign of being corrupt. And unfortunately, I do not believe that the word "corrupt" is too strong to describe them.

A core group meeting was held on **12 October 1995** at the children's charity family centre to discuss what was happening and what action was required, with regard to the children. There were several people in attendance: social workers, the family centre staff, Sally's former headmistress, Mrs Phillips, and Mrs Bell, Sally's class teacher from Oldenhurst First School, which Sally had recently left.

Social workers were voicing all their concerns – about how the children were being emotionally and psychologically harmed due to bad parenting.

They used the example of Sally proving to be a quiet, withdrawn, sad and socially isolated child, and said their concerns were based on information given to them by Oldenhurst First School. I obviously took it that the school had contacted social services, so I asked Mrs Bell, who had been Sally's class teacher in her last year at Oldenhurst, "Why didn't you inform Martha and me about these concerns?"

I also queried, "If she was socially withdrawn, why did Sally's school reports show that she worked well in group activities? It said she interacted so well with other children that her constant talking in class could have a distracting effect!"

Apparently, Sally often had to be told to stop talking, a sign that she certainly was not the quiet, isolated, friendless child they were now trying to portray.

Her old class teacher, Mrs Bell, said she had informed us of her concerns but we had not acted upon them.

"When did you voice these concerns?" I asked her and she claimed it had been at the last parents' evening.

"You did not!" I disagreed.

But she remained adamant, saying, "In fact, you were so dismissive that I was seriously concerned about your lack of interest in your own child's welfare. I clearly remember telling you, but you seemed to take little notice. "

My blood boiled, but I kept my head. I knew this was nonsense, and I could prove it. "Parents have to make appointments to see the teachers at parents' evening," I countered, "and if you look at the school records, you will see that Martha and I didn't attend parents' evening. How can you clearly remember telling us your concerns at the last parents' evening when we weren't even there?"

Mrs Bell went bright red in the face and blustered, "Well, then, it must have been the year before."

"The year before?" I replied. "You weren't Sally's class teacher the year before."

Mrs Bell was in a panic. She then said, "Well, if you *had* attended parents' evening, then I would have told you! But as you were not there, then I had no way of informing us."

"So, you're admitting you didn't inform us."

"I *would* have!"

What a difference there is, between "definitely remember talking to you at parents evening" and "I would have talked to you if you had been there"!

The parents' evening that Mrs Bell was referring to would have been the last one before Sally left Oldenhurst to go to middle school. If she had made a genuine mistake about which parents' evening it was, surely she would have said it must have been the previous term, not the previous year. In fact, there was only one parents' evening that year – the other terms were covered by reports. It was obvious that she was not telling the truth and had been caught out, but why was she lying about something as serious as this?

When it was her turn and I asked Mrs Phillips, Oldenhurst's headmistress, why she hadn't discussed with us any perceived problems Sally had, Mrs Phillips said that they preferred to deal with problems within the school itself, if possible.

I frowned. This certainly wasn't being dealt with internally! I addressed Mrs Phillips and asked, "If that's the case, why did you contact social services before trying to contact us, either by phone or post?"

"We didn't." Mrs Phillips said that social services had contacted them with concerns about Sally.

"So, you didn't have sufficient concerns to contact us – let alone social services, but after social services contacted the school, you suddenly had concerns?" I shook my head in disbelief. "Mrs Phillips, why is Sally now being described as a sad and isolated little girl with no friends," I asked, "when four years of school reports described her as a boisterous, talkative girl who does well in team games?"

Before Mrs Phillips could reply, a social worker interrupted and changed the topic of conversation.

About a week after this meeting, Martha and I attended another meeting at the family centre. During the course of this meeting, attended by social worker Carol Foster, centre worker, Linda Berry, and a few other nameless faces, most of the talk was about the children, and how Martha's and my inability to parent correctly was having a detrimental effect on them. Berry indicated that the report she was preparing for court would show that they had serious concerns about our abilities as parents.

After listening to them talking between themselves, I addressed Linda Berry, and in front of all those so-called professionals, I asked her the same question that I had asked her at the time of our first attendance at the centre: "How can you possibly give an impartial assessment without being influenced by the contents of the social services referral letter?"

To my amazement, Berry replied, "What referral letter?"

She denied any knowledge of such a document and claimed that I must have been mistaken. I couldn't believe what I was hearing!

"But it was you, yourself, who showed us the paper!"

But she reiterated that she had no knowledge of its existence.

I think what had happened was that Berry had shown us a referral form that was not meant for our eyes, not realising that the contents aimed to influence the outcome of their assessment. Because the staff at the children's charity family centre were working very closely with social services and depended on them for finance and support, I would imagine that they decided to say that such a referral letter did not exist. It would be the simplest solution: after all, staff could not be influenced by the contents of a non-existent letter.

This only served to reinforce my views that

lying and scheming seemed to come quite easily to them all, and that they were prepared to go to any lengths to achieve their aims. Wouldn't you call this type of behaviour corruption?

John should have had a follow-up appointment with the speech and language therapist in December 1995, but for some reason this never came through. Taking note of what had been said at this last meeting, particularly Linda Berry's comments, I urged the health visitor to arrange another appointment for the children. We received another appointment for **23 January 1996**, at which the speech therapist again said she had no concerns about the children.

By this time, John was attending playschool two mornings a week. I approached the staff there and asked about John and whether they had any concerns about his behaviour. They replied that they had seen nothing to give them any concern.

Sally was now attending Hillsway Middle School. Shortly before a parents' evening in October 1995, Sally had remarked to me how much she liked this school and especially her form teacher, Mr Thomas. When I asked her why, she replied that Mr Thomas did not shout at her or shake her if she was naughty. I carefully asked her what she meant.

She told me that, at Oldenhurst First School, "Mrs Bell would always shout at me to stop talking to my friends. Once, she caught me talking to Lauren and laughing, and Mrs Bell shouted at me and told me to come to the front of the class. Then she shook me really hard by the shoulders till my teeth rattled."

There was Linda Berry from the local family centre, preparing a statement for the court about how damaged Rachel and John were. And Sally's case was documented by a statement from Mrs Bell, describing her as a very sad, quiet, lonely and isolated little girl with no friends within the school!

Now, here was Sally, telling me that this very same teacher had been shaking her and shouting at her for talking and laughing with other children. I looked again at all Sally's school reports from Oldenhurst, and saw that they described her as a child who always thrived within a group and interacted well with others, alarm bells began to ring.

These are the general comments from Sally's end-of-year school reports. The first is from Mrs Bell.

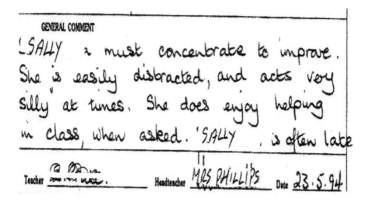

"General Comments – Sally really needs to concentrate more on her work. She wastes a great deal of her time in class and this is reflected in the quality of her work. I'm sure she is capable of producing much better work than she does." Dated 7 June 1995.

Those following are from the two previous years and different teachers:

"General Comments – Sally must concentrate to improve. She is easily distracted, and acts very silly at times. She does enjoy helping in class, when asked. Sally is often late." Dated 23 May 1994.

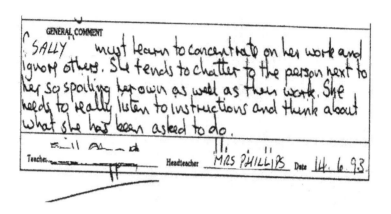

"General Comments – Sally must learn to concentrate on her work and ignore others. She tends to chatter to the person next to her so spoiling her own as well as their work. She needs to really listen to instructions and think about what she has been asked to do." Dated 14 June 1993.

I decided to contact Kathleen Archer from child protection on **28 November 1995** to tell her what Sally had said, and how this information contradicted Mrs Bell's statement.

Archer shrugged it off, saying, "Come on,

Dave."

It seemed she was implying that I had made it up! Either that, or she intended to prevent Sally's remarks being used to challenge Mrs Bell's statement. Whatever the intention was, it put an end to us pursuing Sally's allegations at that time; well, for a few months, anyway.

Chapter 7

At a planning meeting held at the family centre on **15 January 1996**, those present were Carol Foster, a social worker; Kathleen Archer from child protection; Lisa Bridge and Linda Berry from the family centre; Martha and myself. During the meeting, the subject of whose responsibility it was for the problems within the family was raised.

Kathleen Archer stated that responsibility for the welfare of the children falls on the parents. I agreed, but said that if there was a problem within the family that could not be rectified or dealt with within the family, such as a member of the family suffering from mental illness, then responsibility to provide appropriate help and support falls on the local authority.

"I've asked on numerous occasions for help and support for Martha, but any help or assistance has been refused – on the grounds that the parent with the condition did not pose a physical risk to the children!" I wiped the sweat off my brow. I was so tired of having these battles, but they wouldn't prevent me from fighting our corner.

"My opinion," I went on, "is – if there really is

a problem in the family, it's you who are responsible for it. It's due to the failure of social services to provide appropriate support for a person with a mental disorder, when it's been requested!"

Carol Foster, the social worker, said, "I find that hard to believe. I don't think that's true."

I imagine she may have helped to write the referral letter to the family centre which cast me in such a bad light!

I pointed out that their own records would show that in June 1993, Caroline Peterson, the health visitor, had requested psychiatric support for Martha – but that request had been ignored.

The meeting moved on to discuss John's behaviour while at the family centre and the continuing concern of the staff as to why John was quiet and shy in the mornings, but more lively later on in the day. I didn't know what they were hoping to prove – that we psychologically abused him before we set off, and he warmed up to their care in the afternoon? That we drugged him all night and he 'came round' later?

I replied that I thought the comments of the so-called professionals were now moving into the realms of the ridiculous. I also told the meeting that I had asked staff at the playschool that John was now attending if they had any concerns about him and they said none whatsoever.

Kathleen Archer indicated that they required Sally to undergo a psychiatric assessment by a team of specialists headed by Dr Tracy Swinton, a child psychiatrist. The assessment would consist of seven appointments and the first one or two would involve seeing the whole family together.

I swallowed hard. This was such an ordeal – for all the children, as well as for Martha and me. But again, we wanted to be seen to comply – otherwise, we feared the worst.

We all took Sally to the first appointment, which lasted about two hours. We were being asked questions – and when I say "we," I do mean all of us. It was not an interrogation-type situation, but very casual and relaxed. The children were being asked about school and home, and I thought it was done in a way that did not make them feel as if they were being questioned. So, I had no complaints.

Towards the end of the session, Dr Swinton said that they had been in touch with Sally's school and the reports that had come back were describing Sally as a "jolly, bubbly little girl", and that this was very pleasing. Dr Swinton said that she did not believe that Sally had suffered from her home environment and looked forward to seeing the whole family at the next appointment. We breathed a sigh of relief.

Shortly after this meeting, we received a letter from social services saying that Dr Swinton had been taken ill and since it was not known when she would return to work, she would not be able to finish the assessment. We were told that Sally would now be assessed by a psychologist, and that three appointments would be required for the assessment.

I voiced my concerns as to how an individual psychologist could make an accurate assessment in three appointments, when a team of child psychiatrists felt that at least seven were required to make an accurate assessment – not just of Sally, but of the interaction of the whole family.

I contacted Kathleen Archer and said I was not happy with the situation. I was worried that this psychologist was not a child specialist, which I felt the situation required.

I did not tell Archer this, but I felt the assessment by Dr Swinton's team had been terminated because it was showing positive results. I said I would have to consider whether or not to allow Sally to see a psychologist, as I believed a child psychiatrist was better qualified.

The following day, I received a letter informing me that if I did not cooperate, an assessment order would be sought. We had no choice.

Psychologist Kelly Andrews saw Sally on three occasions and some time after the third and final appointment, we were informed of the outcome of her assessment. The psychologist stated that, based on the three meetings with Sally and with access to the witness statement by school teacher Mrs Bell, in her opinion, Sally had been seriously damaged and would continue to be damaged if she remained in the family home!

We were desperate. Martha withdrew into her shell, preparing for the worst again. I tried to address the matter head-on, but I needed to explore all possibilities. I might be clutching at straws, but there was no way I would give up Sally – or any of our children – without a fight.

This report made no mention of contacting the school Sally had, by now, been attending for four months, and there was no mention of Sally's accusations of assault against Mrs Bell. And yet, the previous team of psychiatrists had contacted

Hillsway Middle School, and what a different picture was being painted: "a jolly, bubbly little girl"!

In my opinion, Kelly Andrews, the psychologist, could not make an accurate and true assessment because she had only been given selected information from social services to study: no up-to-date information from Sally's present school and no information about Sally's accusation of assault by her former teacher, Mrs Bell. I know that I had only mentioned Sally's accusations briefly to Kathleen Archer, but I thought that it would have been looked into, not just shrugged off.

I am sure that if Sally had told the teacher that a parent had assaulted her, social services would have had us in court before we had time to put our coats on. No, social services were determined to find damaged children and prove that the parents were to blame.

At a parents' evening at Hillsway Middle School on **7 March 1996,** I spoke to Sally's class teacher, Mr Thomas. I asked him how Sally was getting on, and whether he was aware of our involvement with social services.

He told me he was aware that social services were involved with the family. He also said that for the first day or two at the school, Sally had appeared quiet and reserved, but she soon seemed to perk up and by the end of her first week, she was a fully confident little girl, sometimes to the point of being silly. She had lots of friends and he noted that she interacted very well.

Mr Thomas said the school had been informed about Sally on her arrival at the school but he said that Sally's improvement was so rapid from Day One that he wondered if the main problem was merely that Sally had not been happy at her previous school. This comment made me think again about Sally's allegation about Mrs Bell.

The next morning, I asked Sally to tell me exactly what had happened with Mrs Bell at Oldenhurst First School. Sally said that she had been talking to Lauren, one of her friends in class, and Mrs Bell shouted at her to stop talking. A few minutes later she began talking again, and when Mrs Bell heard her, Sally was told to come to the front of the classroom where Mrs Bell gripped her by both upper arms and shook her violently, shouting, "When I tell you to stop talking, you will stop talking!"

Sally said that when she went back to her seat, James Sparrow, the boy sat next to her, whispered, "Teachers are not supposed to do that to children."

Sally told me that when Mrs Bell was shaking her she was pushing her thumbs into Sally's arms and that her arms had hurt for the rest of the day. She said that afterwards, the whole class had gone very quiet.

After hearing this, I felt that I had no option but to complain officially to Oldenhurst First School, so I sent a written complaint on **13 March 1996**. A week later, I received a reply from Mrs Phillips, the headmistress, saying that she had spoken to Kathleen Archer from child protection about the incident.

They had agreed between themselves that, due to pressures of work, and the fact that Sally would be involved in child protection procedures in the near future, that they would defer talking about this incident until later in the year, after the court hearing! However, Mrs Phillips intimated that she would continue to deal with it as an internal matter within the school.

I found this reply unbelievable considering the emphasis that social services were placing on Mrs Bell's witness statement about Sally being an isolated, damaged little girl, whilst at the same time disregarding the comments of Hillsway Middle School, who had continually told me that Sally was a bubbly, happy little child!

I was struggling to comprehend the lack of logic in the situation. Kathleen Archer had written a report stating that Sally was seriously emotionally damaged due to bad parenting, had no friends and was totally isolated from her peers at school with no identity of her own. Archer's report was largely based on a statement from Sally's previous school teacher, Mrs Bell, who Sally now indicated she was frightened of, after being assaulted by her for talking in class.

Was I missing something? Sally was being made out to be a totally isolated child, without friends, without an identity of her own, but she had been physically shaken in front of the class for persistent talking to other children. Surely anyone could see that something did not add up: a child who does not talk is physically punished for talking in class?

I would have thought Kathleen Archer, being a child protection worker, would have wanted to investigate the assault allegation. But no, it would appear that Mrs Phillips, Oldenhurst's head mistress, Archer and team leader, Suzie Ralph, had decided between themselves that Sally was not to be interviewed about the assault allegation. The reason given was that they had "concluded that it was not a child protection issue", and it "was of a relatively minor nature and could not be substantiated by medical or other evidence".

In another response to the accusation, it was stated that it would be merely the child's word against the teacher's, so there was no point in pursuing the matter by talking to Sally about it.

Mrs Phillips wrote that her views were the same as other professionals involved with the case: the accusations of assault were merely an attempt by myself, Mr Jordan, to discredit the main witness, Mrs Bell. I do not know how this would appear to other people, but to me, it seemed as if a conspiracy had taken place between Mrs Phillips, Kathleen Archer and Suzie Ralph, to prevent an accusation of an assault on a child from being appropriately investigated.

To me, this is a crime in itself, and to make it even more vile, it would appear that the conspirators deliberately intended to never interview Sally about the assault, purely to enable them to use Mrs Bell's statement for the purpose of removing Sally from her home.

If Sally or any of her classmates had been interviewed and confirmed that the teacher had shaken Sally, where would that have left social services' evidence of a child damaged due to bad parenting? And what would have happened to the teacher's reputation and career?

We had been told by Kathleen Archer that the local authority would be applying to the court to have Sally removed from the family home because of how damaged she was, due to her treatment at home. We were devastated – and I could not believe the injustice of this. It was a vendetta!

I told Archer, "I thought social services tried to work with families and offered help to keep children in their homes! What are you doing – taking ours away?"

"We usually try to, but in your case, removal of the children is the only option," she said.

"Why?"

"We can't work with you because you have deceived us in the past and you distort facts."

"It's not me that distorts facts," I said. "It's you social workers that do that."

Here are a few extracts taken from documents related to the complaint I made regarding Mrs Bell's alleged assault on Sally (names have been changed).

The first is the main body of the letter from Mrs Phillips, the headmistress, to me, dated 19 March 1996:

Dear Mr. Jordan,

Further to our telephone conversation this morning.

I have spoke to MS ARCHER / Social Worker, and we have agreed that due to pressure of work and to the fact that SALLY ⸱ will be involved in protection procedures in the near future we shall defer a meeting with SALLY until the middle of May at the earliest.

Your comments have been noted and the matter will be pursued within school as appropriate.

After this reply from the school, I made a formal complaint to the local authority, stating that, in my view, the accusation of assault should have been investigated immediately. The local authority agreed to carry out an investigation, but that did not take place until two years later (1 June 1998).

On **20 March 1996** Kathleen Archer and

Carol Foster, a social worker, came to our house and presented us with a work plan they had drawn up for Sally. This work plan basically told us which social worker would be working with Sally at what times, talking about various subjects to do with Sally's life. The real purpose was to try to get information from Sally that social services could use to help them obtain a care order in court.

I knew that if I said no to them outright, they would be in court within days, seeking a court order. To buy time to think, I told them that I would need time to study their work plan, so Archer said she would phone me the next day to get my agreement. I saw that there was one aspect of Sally's life that was missing, and felt that this should be discussed.

Archer phoned the next day as promised. "You've had time to look at it, now. Do you agree to the plan?"

I said, "Before agreeing, I'd like it to include talking to Sally about the assault by the teacher at Oldenhurst First School."

"No! Certainly not!"

"It's a serious matter that impacts on her life, and I feel it should be discussed."

Archer became indignant, telling me she

would not alter the plan and that the incident at Oldenhurst was "...insignificant, compared to the ten years of neglect and abuse Sally's suffered at home!"

I seethed but kept my cool. She seemed to be trying to provoke me, so I ignored her attack and persisted. "It is an allegation of assault, nevertheless. Surely that should be a topic of discussion about aspects of her life? You mention everything else – friends, hobbies, school..."

"As far as I'm concerned," Archer snapped, "it's a school matter, anyway. Not a concern of the child protection team."

"How can you consider an assault on a child to be 'insignificant'?" I asked her. "How can it be 'of no concern' to you? Isn't it about protecting a child? Aren't you 'child protection'?"

All Archer said to this was: "If you have a complaint, put it in writing."

She demanded to know if I agreed to their work plan.

"I will if the assault issue is included."

"No," Archer said. "I will contact our legal department as I am taking your reply to be a refusal." And she put the phone down on me.

On many occasions, these so-called

professionals can be anything but professional.

Later the same day, I was contacted by our solicitor who had been informed by social services that the local authority would be applying for an interim care order on **25 March 1996,** because I was refusing to allow Kathleen Archer to work with Sally. After some discussion with the solicitor, I said that I would allow Archer to work with Sally, but that I was not happy with the situation.

I was not happy at all about Archer or the way she worked. She was giving the impression that she believed the children were in a damaging situation and that they needed to be removed from the family home as soon as possible. And yet, here is a list of appointments she made to see Sally, all of which I kept a note of from her first encounter:

- *4 October 1995: Archer due to work with Sally within school at 3.15 p.m. Archer phoned shortly before appointment and said there had been strike action, so she was now behind in her work and she would have to cancel*

the appointment as other things took
priority.

- 30 October 1995: Archer due to work

  with Sally at 3.15 p.m. At 3.30 p.m.

  school phoned social services, as Archer

  had not arrived. She arrived at

  3.52 p.m., 37 minutes late.

- 9 November 1995: Archer due to work

  with Sally at 3.15 p.m. Archer phoned

  earlier that day to say she could not

  make it, and would see Sally on 10

  November at 3.15 p.m. instead.

- 10 November 1995: Archer due to work

  with Sally at 3.15 p.m. Archer phoned

  earlier in the day to say she could not

  make it, and would see Sally on 13

November at 3.15 p.m. instead.

- 13 November 1995: Archer due to work with Sally at 3.15 p.m. Archer did not phone the school to cancel, but did not turn up for the appointment, so the school phoned social services and were told there had been a mix up and she would see Sally on 14 November instead.

- 14 November 1995: Archer arrived to see Sally at 3.15 p.m. Made another appointment for 16 November.

- 16 November 1995: Archer arrived to see Sally at 3.15 p.m. Made another appointment for 23 November.

- 23 November 1995: Archer arrived to see Sally at 3.15 p.m. Made another appointment for 28 November.

- 28 November 1995: Archer arrived to see Sally at 3.15 p.m. Earlier that day, I phoned Archer to tell her that Sally had told me about her previous teacher Mrs Bell shaking her in front of the class for laughing and talking, I referred to it as an assault. This is when Archer replied, "Come on, Dave." She was basically accusing me of making it up. Archer said she would see Sally the following day, 29 November, so I told her to talk to Sally about it, but Archer refused.

- 29 November 1995: Archer due to work with Sally at 3.15 p.m. Archer phoned earlier that day to say she could not make it and would see Sally on 4

December.

- 4 December 1995: Archer due to work

  with Sally at 3.15 p.m. Archer phoned at

  2.45 p.m., saying she could not make it

  but would take Sally out for food at

  4 p.m. on 20 December.

- 20 December 1995: Archer phoned in

  the morning to say she could not take

  Sally out as she was now taking a girl to

  Leamington Spa.

- 12 January 1996: Archer took Sally

  for food after school.

Out of a total of fourteen appointments, seven (50
per cent) were cancelled.

Chapter 8

We were now facing a two-pronged attack: a child protection worker and social services were trying to build enough evidence to allow them to go to court for a care order to remove Sally from the home, while the children's charity family centre staff and social services were trying to compile enough evidence to remove Rachel and John from the home as well!

From the outside, you would think we must have done terrible things to the children. The reality was, we hadn't. But this stress and distress was tearing us apart, and Martha was fragile enough. Yet, the children were never, ever affected by her difficulties. She poured love on them and did the best she could – she was just struggling, and this situation only made things worse. I did my best, too. And I was coming out fighting.

We attended a meeting at the family centre and there were the usual people there: Kathleen Archer, Carol Foster, Linda Berry and another woman I had not seen before. This new person was introduced as Jan Berkley-Grey, another social worker. She looked completely different from all the very stern and very white social workers that we had encountered so far: she was a black woman with braided hair and a brightly coloured top, and she even had a smile on her face! We were told that Berkley-Grey was to work with Sally during school hours. I asked what they meant by "work with Sally" and was told it was to talk to Sally about her past – Sally's "life story", as Berkley-Grey referred to it. The intention was to find out how Sally's life had affected her, and what support she would need in the future.

As Berkley-Grey had never met Sally, she indicated that she would like to first see Sally in her home environment before meeting her in school. It was arranged that Berkley-Grey would meet Sally at home on **19 April 1996,** after school, at 4.30 p.m.

I was at work when Jan Berkley-Grey visited the house, so when I got home I immediately asked how the meeting had gone. All three children said they liked Berkley-Grey a lot. They said she told them funny stories and made them laugh, and she played with them and let them touch her hair.

"Why did she let you touch her hair?" I asked.

They replied "Because we've never seen

someone with hair like that before!"

I asked Martha and the children if Berkley-Grey had said anything about the family, before leaving.

Martha told me, "Well, just before she left, she said she could see nothing wrong with the children and that they seemed perfectly happy at home. She said she couldn't see what all the concern was about!"

I raised my eyebrows. That was a turn-up for the books!

She had left telling them that she would see Sally at school on **3 May 1996**.

The day came for Jan Berkley-Grey to work with Sally at school, but she phoned the school just before the appointment to cancel and rearranged it for **17 May 1996**.

After school on the day of the new appointment, I asked Sally how the meeting had gone. Sally said that Berkley-Grey had not turned up, so I phoned the school to ask what had happened. The headmistress was unaware that Berkley-Grey had not attended because the school had not been notified of any cancellation. The headmistress phoned social services and another appointment was made.

When Berkley-Grey was next at the school to see Sally, she brought a cake with her. Sally said they shared the cake and Berkley-Grey was telling her things to make her laugh – also, talking about Kathleen Archer and laughing.

I am not sure if they were laughing about how Archer looked or how she acted, or both, but it did seem unusual that a social worker would allow a fellow professional to be the topic of humour. All the social workers we had been involved with stuck together and would never give differing views of a colleague.

Berkley-Grey told Sally that the cake was a little going-away present, because she was going back to Birmingham. It was not clear if she was going back to Birmingham to work, or to live, but she said she would not be able to see Sally again.

It seemed too much of a coincidence that Berkley-Grey had given the opinion that she had no concern regarding the family – and the next time she saw her, she was leaving, without finishing her assigned task. It made me think of the psychiatrist Dr Swinton and her team: she had also said she thought the children were not suffering at home, and consequently disappeared without finishing the work she had been assigned.

As social services were trying to compile enough evidence to apply to the court for a care order on Sally, a *guardian ad litem* was assigned to her. The guardian was a social worker brought in from outside the area, who was supposed to be totally independent and work solely in Sally's best interests.

On one occasion, during a meeting at the house, the guardian, Patricia Hughes, sighed, sat back in her seat, and said, "It seems that social services' view and your view are totally polarised. It's obviously not going to be possible for anything constructive to come out of a situation like this."

"Tell me about it," I said, frustrated.

She shook her head as if I was a lost cause, which just riled me even more.

"How are we ever going to NOT be in conflict? You tell me how we're ever going to meet in the middle! Kathleen Archer's already said that social workers can't work with me, and their only option is to apply to remove the children from the home!"

Patricia Hughes indicated that unless I began to agree with social services' view of events, then she, the supposedly independent guardian, would have to side with social services!

I frowned. "So, this is you, basically saying you're independent only as long as I agree with everything social services are saying and go along with it? How independent is that?"

"I didn't say that," she said, her lips tight.

"Not gonna happen." I shook my head, my arms folded. "I can't possibly agree with what the "SS" are saying – because, in my opinion, they are wrong!"

Yes, I did refer to social services as the "SS", and the guardian did not like it one bit.

The normal procedure for social services is to keep children within the home, if possible, and work with the parents to improve the situation. If social services were not prepared to do this, they would have to have a very good reason to put before the court.

The guardian's next visit to our house was again to try to get me to admit our failings as parents and to go along with what social services wanted. Again, I told the guardian that because the only course of action social services were prepared to take was to remove the children, I had no option but to challenge them all the way.

Patricia Hughes, the guardian, took out of her

briefcase a copy of a statement she had prepared that was to be used at court, and let me read it. It was mainly just mirroring the social services reports, but she had also stated that social services were unable to work with me because I had deceived them in the past!

I gasped, incredulous. "When did I deceive social services?" I asked.

"When you allowed Martha to have access to Sally after you'd been granted custody in September 1988," Hughes answered. She said, "Custody had only been granted to you on the understanding that Martha was never to be allowed access to Sally."

"At the custody hearing, the magistrates, in fact, allowed access between Martha and Sally!" I replied. "So I did *not* deceive social services in any way!"

Hughes claimed that I must have been mistaken.

"I clearly remember it! A helpful ex-barrister asked the court to allow Martha access," I insisted.

Patricia looked me straight in the eye and said, "David, a court would not have done that."

Was she accusing me of being mistaken, or of simply lying?

"Excuse me. Wait a moment," I told her.

I went upstairs to where I keep important papers, one of which was a copy of the custody order I had held onto, all those years. I thundered downstairs and gave it to Hughes to read.

You should have seen her face when she got to the part that stated Martha was to have access to Sally!

"So – how, exactly, have I deceived social services, when I was simply complying with the instructions on the custody order?" I asked her.

Fuming with humiliation, she left.

Several days later, Hughes returned with an amended court statement and asked me to read it to check for any inaccuracies.

I didn't know at the time, but I suspect the real reason that Hughes and social services were letting me read their court statement was so that I would show them which parts of their statements I would be able to challenge them on. They would then be able to amend the statements, taking out the inaccuracies – or dare I say it, the "bare-faced lies" – that I knew to be false and could disprove. I think they wanted to submit statements based solely on things I was not aware of, or wasn't able to disprove.

Why would I have this view? Well, every expert or professional involved with the case who gave a positive assessment towards the family quickly vanished from the scene. What does that tell you?

The new statement by Patricia Hughes claimed that I had acquired a council property using deception! And that my deception had been exposed, and I was subsequently evicted!

"This is ridiculous! I have never been evicted," I told her. "How could you put such a thing in a court statement?"

"Details of the eviction are in our records," she said, "and I'm only putting in the statement what is in the records about you."

I almost laughed. Evicting someone from a council property is not something a council can do easily, especially if you have what is called a secure tenancy, which is what I had. I told Patricia that I had never been evicted and if it stated that in their records then their records were wrong.

It was clear that they were trying to show that I was of bad character. First, they said I had deceived them because I allowed access between Martha and Sally and this was against my agreement with them! But after I showed them that a court had ordered this access, this attempt to discredit me was removed from the statement – only to be replaced with this mythical tale of eviction, due to acquiring a property using deception! Now I had to prove their claims to be false. Again.

I contacted Bradford Common Council and was told that their housing was now run by a housing association, so I would need to contact them, for details of any eviction because they now held all the housing records.

I phoned the housing association and gave a brief explanation of my situation. The housing association told me they had no details of any eviction in their records and confirmed that any court action resulting in an eviction is kept on file.

"Thanks. Could you send me a letter stating this, please?" I asked the woman on the phone.

And this, she did. When I received a copy of the letter, I showed it to Patricia Hughes, and very soon a new statement had been drawn up, with any mention of eviction removed.

I later found out from some local authority letters what it was that social services referred to as an "eviction". Bradford Common housing department had once written to me stating the date on which I had to vacate the property I was in at the time. But this was not an eviction: it was the fact that I had entered into a mutual exchange agreement and it had taken longer to complete the exchange than it should have. The letter was merely informing me that I needed to vacate the property by a certain date, because my tenancy of the new property would start on that same date. Far from an eviction!

Somehow, Bankham social services had gained access to details pertaining to me, held at a Bradford Common housing association, and had taken certain words out of context to make it appear that I had been evicted! This is the sort of deceit and underhand behaviour Bankham social services were capable of.

Social services knew that I was conscious of how far they would twist and distort things – and they were also well-aware that I was going to fight them all the way!

"Because social services and you disagree on the well-being of the children, especially Sally," Kathleen Archer said, "if you were to agree to allow a voluntary care order to be placed on Sally, this would allow us to see how Sally is, for ourselves."

"Not on your life!" was my instant reply.

But my solicitor suggested that this was the only way we would resolve this problem. They would obviously not let this go without some kind of concession to their demands.

"That's going too far!" I exclaimed.

The solicitor was vehement. I was advised to let social services see for themselves that Sally was not this damaged child they claimed she was.

After much thought and discussion, trying to alleviate much of the decision-making from Martha in her fragile state, I reluctantly indicated that I would agree. But only if they said that Sally would remain at her current school and would not be moved. She needed some security in her life, for however short this 'proof' period would be. Archer said that they had no intention of moving Sally to another school, and that it was important for Sally's life to remain as stable as possible.

So, like a stupid fool, I agreed.

Chapter 9

Some days later, we were asked to attend a meeting at the family centre to discuss Sally going to foster parents. At that meeting, there was a haughty woman from the foster parents' association. I could tell that she liked to think she was superior to the "service user" and I got the feeling she didn't have much of a liking for me. I couldn't imagine why. She'd never met me before.

She asked, "What have you done to prepare Sally for going to foster parents? Have you explained to her what's going to happen?"

I replied, "Yes, I've explained it to Sally, in an age-appropriate manner."

Her lip twisted in a barely-concealed sneer. I could tell that she didn't want to hear words like that. Those were the sort of words social workers use – the words she wanted to say to me.

She had really wanted me to reveal that I'd told Sally everything that was about to happen. And then she could say to me, "NO, David! You must tell her in an *age-appropriate manner*!"

Because I had appropriated and used their terminology and because she still had to somehow show that I was wrong, she said, instead, "NO, David! You should have told her everything! You should have explained absolutely everything to her – all about what's gone wrong in the family!"

I disagreed with her and said I felt that an explanation must be given in an age-appropriate manner.

"No, you must explain *every* detail to a child," she insisted.

"So, you're telling me that if a child is to go into hospital for an operation," I said, "you would tell them every single thing that is going to happen to them?"

"Yes," she nodded firmly.

"Well, you have shocked me," I replied. "I would tell them in an age-appropriate manner. I'd say something like, 'you'll go into hospital, and the doctor will make you go to sleep, and when you wake up, you will be better'." I looked at her askance. "You're telling me you'd tell a child all the gory details, and almost certainly traumatise them?"

She gave me such a nasty look. "I'm not stopping in the same room as this person!" she raged, before storming out.

I found that virtually all the social workers

who were involved with the case seemed to work along the same lines: they had to show you that you were wrong – or were going wrong. It must have been obvious to them, really: if there's nothing wrong with you, what are you doing there, in the first place?

Whenever you give an analysis of a situation, they have to say the opposite, to show you that you're wrong. This means they often fall into traps of their own making. The biggest problem with social workers – and probably the scariest thing – is that they cannot even contemplate the possibility that they may have made a mistake, so they will do whatever is necessary to support their actions. If that means distorting facts, they will distort facts. If it means telling lies, they will tell lies. They think they are right, so the outcome justifies the means.

On **26 June 1996,** a voluntary interim care order was granted. What a big mistake I made in allowing this!

After the interim care order had been granted, we were not allowed to see Sally for about a month. Social services said that this was because Sally did not want to see her family.

Now they had placed Sally with foster

parents, they could describe her in whatever way they wanted, and of course – they concluded that she was a 'very damaged child'. Based on the assessment made while she was in foster care, they said that social services would be applying for a full care order.

When we were eventually allowed to see Sally, it was with a social worker and the foster parents in attendance, and gradually, this progressed to just the foster parents bringing Sally to our house for visits.On one occasion at our house, while Sally was playing with Rachel and John, I asked her foster parents what they thought about Sally, and whether she was the damaged little girl the social workers had been describing.

They said, " She most definitely is not!"

From the first day Sally entered their home, they said they had never seen the damaged little girl the social workers described. They told us she had always been a happy, normal young girl!

"But if you've never seen her as a damaged little girl, how can social workers be describing her like this?" I asked them, in bewilderment. "Don't they ask you about her? And will you be asked to make a statement for the court, describing your views of Sally?"

The foster parents said no, they had not been asked to make a statement.

I could have thought we were both going mad. Certainly, Martha was driven in that direction by the whole terrible, long, drawn-out affair. But I had straws to clutch – in terms of real, trustworthy people who couldn't see what social services claimed. That kept my sanity, through the terrible times – clinging onto the truth. It was still very worrying when sensible, level-headed people such as Sally's middle school teacher, Mr Thomas; the psychiatric nurse, Sharon Fowler, and the speech and language therapist were all saying they could see nothing wrong with the children – and yet social services disregarded the opinions of these people. The foster parents who had been caring for Sally for some months were not even asked for their opinion! I would imagine that if the foster parents had voiced a very negative opinion about Sally, social services would have asked them to give a court statement in no time at all.

During our normal week, we not only had visits from social workers and the guardian, all checking up on us – but also from the children's charity staff, Linda Berry and Lisa Bridge. They would monitor everything that went on while they were at the house, and it would all be written up into a report. Even ordinary activities would be documented in such a way as to make them appear unusual – and an indication that there were problems in the family. If the children were laughing and playing, they would be considered 'out of control'. If they were quiet, they were considered to be 'subdued'. Anything was interpreted in such a way as to make the children's normal behaviour seem abnormal.

A good example of this was on **7 October 1996**. It was one of the many meetings that were arranged to discuss the family situation, and the usual people were there: social workers, the children's charity family centre staff and various other local authority personnel. Everyone in the room was given a copy of a report that would have been made by a social worker or one of the family centre staff. On this occasion, it was a report written by Linda Berry from the family centre. The report contained the usual derogatory garbage, saying a lot – and at the same time, saying nothing.

I was reading it, and a couple of things caught my eye, so I waited until a "professional" was talking – in this case, it was Sandra Watkins, the chairperson. I interrupted her in mid-speech to query something.

I always liked to interrupt them mid-speech (politely, of course) as I had found that if you interrupted them, it was very easy to break their train of thought. Due to the fact that there were usually at least six of them against us, it did help to even the playing field a little.

I drew Watkins' attention to an apparent contradiction in the report.

"In one paragraph," I pointed out on the sheet, and all their heads went down to read. "It says that 'John was observed going to the fridge and taking a drink from a bottle'. You say that John had supposedly not asked permission from his parents – and that this apparently showed a complete lack of boundaries. However, later – on page 3, you state that 'Rachel was observed asking her parents if she could have a biscuit to eat', and you speculate that 'if Rachel felt comfortable in her home environment, she would not have felt the need to ask permission'."

I looked over at Linda Berry, who had written the report, and said, "John didn't ask permission, and you say that is wrong. Rachel asked permission, and you say that is wrong. Can you tell me what you think is right?"

I posed this question with a curious, yet concerned look on my face, and in a way that made it appear that Berry was the one being scrutinised and whose ability and competence were in question.

"Well..." she began stuttering. "I... I would have thought..."

It was obvious that she could not give a valid reason for her comments and she didn't have to try, because after only one or two seconds of her blustering, the others moved in quickly to change the subject.

When all the other people in the room close ranks to support each other, there is very little you can do without actually raising your voice. If I was ever to do such a thing, though, I would have been reported as 'being aggressive'. I had to use great skill and walk a fine line just to keep my cool while battling against the odds. In such emotive situations, it was almost impossible.

Berry's report also stated that she had some serious concerns about Martha's and my parenting abilities.

Naturally, I asked Berry, "Please can you tell me what your concerns are? If I understand them, and I agree that your concerns show that we need to do better, then Martha and I can work on our parenting skills to improve on them."

In retrospect, it is almost laughable. I could embellish on it now, if I wanted to. I could say that I looked at her with a pure and innocent gaze, then gave a low bow and an elaborate flourish of the arms and asked, "Pray tell, Madam, how we may appease your majesties?" But it was no laughing matter at the time. I had no time or will for playing games with them. And yet, ironically, it was some kind of game to them. And it seemed to require more concentration, intellectual challenge and manoeuvring than the toughest of chess matches or world war battle plans.

Berry stated that: "My concerns are that you do not accept that you have any parenting problems."

I nodded. I couldn't argue with that. And yet – was that a parenting problem?

"And also – you are domineering. You always speak for Martha and you don't allow her to have her say."

"You're right. I don't believe Martha and I have serious parenting problems," I disputed her claims, saying, "And as for me talking on Martha's behalf... Well, I would have thought it is obvious that because she is on heavy medication, she finds it difficult to answer questions or to reply adequately to some of the ridiculous allegations that have been put to us!"

They all sat with pursed lips, a couple of them making notes – or perhaps they were doodling. Who knew?

Again, I asked Berry, "If you do have valid concerns about our parenting – then, could you please tell me what your concerns are?"

Berry said, "Your problem is exactly what you have just said! That you don't think that you have parenting problems."

By this point, I was getting a little confused and my head was pounding, so I said to Berry, "I *know* I don't believe we have parenting problems. So, tell me *exactly* what you have concerns about. What have you based this report on? As far as I can see, you're saying that just because we believe we have normal parenting ability – that, in itself, makes us bad parents!"

"Well, on one occasion the children were observed walking about in the house while eating a sandwich," Berry said. "And I don't think that is appropriate behaviour...!

"That is absolutely ridiculous!" I cried, trying to contain my exasperation.

I scanned all their faces as I told the meeting, "I could understand her having concerns if the children were taking things from the fridge and throwing them about on the floor! Or emptying bottles of pop everywhere! But the children don't do that sort of thing! They're well behaved!"

Berry had gone quiet, as had all the other people in the room.

Sandra Watkins, the chair, turned to me and said, "Well, let's move on. The concern about your parenting abilities is not a topic to be discussed at this time, and this meeting should continue..."

"The very purpose of this meeting is to discuss problems within the family!" I pointed out to Watkins. "And Linda Berry's report is likely to be used in court against us! Of course, it's relevant for discussion!"

"This meeting is to discuss the course of action needed to safeguard the children's welfare," Watkins replied. "If you want to discuss Miss Berry's concerns with her, then you should do it later, at the family centre."

"But the children's welfare is down to our parenting ability. And if you're not prepared to discuss our parenting ability, then what is the purpose of this meeting, if the real concerns are not going to be talked about?" I said.

This was feeling like Alice Through the Looking Glass – with everyone talking in riddles and getting nowhere.

I went on: "Linda Berry is to supply a report to the court that is to be used against us. And if she has put in the report that she has concerns about Martha's and my ability as parents – then, I have a right to know what those concerns are, so that I'm able to respond to them."

Watkins then turned to me and said, "David, you have become repetitive. We are going to move on with this meeting. And if you continue along this path, you will be asked to leave the room and I will report that you became obstructive and uncooperative."

I took a breath. "If this is the case," I replied, "then I will say no more on the subject – other than to point out that, at this meeting and in Linda Berry's report, Martha and I have been accused of having serious parenting problems, But we have been prevented from knowing what the concerns are, thus denying us the right to defend ourselves against the accusations."

Later that evening, I wrote a formal letter of complaint to the local authority, detailing all that had occurred at the meeting. I explained that to deliberately prevent us from defending ourselves was, in my opinion, a violation of our human rights.

Receipt of my letter was acknowledged, and I was told that my complaint would be dealt with, in due course.

To confuse matters even further, my comments from this meeting were recorded in the minutes from another child protection conference held on **24 April 1997**. I eventually received a copy of these minutes on **4 September 1997**! It took five months for those minutes to arrive! After reading the minutes, I noticed that a comment I had made had been altered.

It was originally: "If the children did such things as throw things from the fridge or empty bottles of pop onto the floor, then I could understand there being concern, but the children did not do such things – as they are, in general, well behaved."

This had been reported in the minutes as: "… but David states that he did try to control the children if they threw things out of the fridge onto the floor, for instance."

I wrote to Sandra Watkins on **19 September 1997** to inform her of this error and note that it had been recorded in such a way as to give totally false information.

I received a reply from Watkins on **23 September 1997** saying, "I would not alter minutes at this late date, but I will put a note in the file."

It made me wonder if sending out the minutes of a meeting five months late was intended to deliberately prevent any errors in them from being corrected. Suppose months, or even years later, I was to ask for details of a meeting that had been incorrectly recorded. Do you think there would be a copy of the letter I had sent attached? I very much doubt it. There would just be their incorrect version of accounts. Was this deliberate corruption?

Back in the autumn of 1996, I had been telling Martha's psychiatric nurse, Sharon Fowler, about the various meetings that were held by social services and the sort of things that went on at these meetings.

Sharon said, "Ooh. I've never been to such a meeting. Would you and Martha mind if I came along to one?"

We didn't mind at all. In fact, Martha was glad and grateful. And since Sharon was Martha's nurse, who administered Martha's medication at home on many occasions, I couldn't see social services objecting to her coming along with us.

I told her, "Well, then, I'll tell social services you'd like to attend. And when they give us the next meeting date. I'll let you know."

"Great!" she smiled.

I wished I had her enthusiasm.

Social services said that they had no objection and when the next meeting was arranged, they would send a letter to Sharon to notify her.

When the next meeting came, Martha and I attended, and Sharon Fowler was also there. It progressed much as all the other meetings did: mainly rubbish and twaddle. But then, when one of the social workers mentioned how damaged the children were, Sharon piped up.

"Excuse me! I've been to the home many times when the children have been present, and at no time have I seen anything to cause me any concern!" She added that the children appeared completely normal and happy at home!

One of the social workers replied, "With all due respect, you are qualified to deal with people with mental health problems. We are qualified to recognise and deal with child abuse."

Sharon gaped, wide eyed, and stopped in her tracks.

During the meeting, I was scrutinising the latest report that had been given to us, when I spotted something. I squinted at the bottom of the sheet and frowned. *What?* I felt a cold blast of shock hit me, followed quickly by a rush of heat and humiliation.

There was a printed footer containing the document reference and name of the electronic database where the documents were stored. Among the various slashes and characters were the words "Mega Pig".

I'm not having THAT!

I said to Sandra Watkins, the chairperson, "What's this database name on the bottom of the document?"

And before she even looked at it she said blithely, "Oh, just ignore it. That shouldn't have been printed."

"Well, if the file name 'Mega Pig' is in any way referring to me, then it's obvious that it's not meant for my eyes," I answered. "And it's obvious that it shouldn't have been printed."

There was silence in the room as everyone looked at the bottom of the document.

Sandra Watkins looked surprised and said, "No, this is not referring to you. It's just the file name within the database."

"'Mega Pig' is a very strange name to call a folder," I said, in a disbelieving tone, "– unless it's for a derogatory reason."

I hope it was clear to social services that I felt only contempt for them and the way they dealt with people – especially people they thought couldn't stand up for themselves. I'm sure they felt the same about me – resentful and contemptuous – otherwise, why would they name the file on my family "Mega Pig"?

There was no logical reason for it. It didn't bear any resemblance to our family name, or to parts of any of the children or professionals' names involved, or the titles of departments involved. There was no excuse to call a family folder "Mega Pig" for reference. It smacked of something personal to me. It was somebody's cruel, dismissive name for me or Martha. And I was disgusted.

Can you imagine any other professional body referring to a service user as "Mega Pig"? Yes, bad enough they refer to us wholesale as "service users", but I think "victim" would be a more appropriate description in this case. Although I imagine that people who haven't been on the receiving end of social services would probably disagree with me.

Shortly before the meeting finished, Martha and I were asked to leave the room for a few minutes to allow the "professionals" to discuss the case.

After the meeting had finished, Martha and I met up with Sharon Fowler and Sharon told us how shocked she had been with what had taken place.

"I *cannot* believe such things go on!" she cried. "All I can... liken it to... is a modern-day witch-hunt! It's like something you think only happened hundreds of years ago!"

Sharon asked me, "How did you manage to sit there quietly while they were insulting you?" Her eyes blazed with righteous indignation on my behalf. "That's what they were doing! Insulting you! Purposefully – to try to make you angry. Yes! That's it! They were trying to make you angry so you'd start shouting, and then they'd have said you were aggressive or violent – so you would have lost the children instantly!"

"I know what they try to do," I replied, softly.

"But I'm used to it. And it's *me* that makes *them* angry."

"Oh, Dave," she said, her eyes glistening, almost tearful. "I'm so sorry."

I wrote an official complaint about the file name, saying that I believed it was referring to me, and I found this rude and unprofessional. The response I received simply claimed that the file name was not referring to me. I don't doubt that they changed the file name shortly afterwards.

A week or so after the meeting, we received a copy of the summary of the meeting. During the few minutes that Martha and I had been asked to leave the room, it seemed that the people at the meeting had voted on whether or not they had concerns about the family. All present indicated that they had serious concerns, except Sharon Fowler, who, the report said, had abstained.

Chapter 10

I had to find someone to give evidence to contradict their damning statements against us. So, I thought it would be a good idea to try to get a social worker to write a favourable report, to help to counter all the negative ones coming from those involved in our case. The only social worker to have given a favourable view of us was Jan Berkley-Grey, so I decided to contact her. But first I had to find her.

Now, the last I had heard about Jan Berkley-Grey was when she had gone to Hillsway Middle School to tell Sally she would no longer be working with her on Sally's life story and that she was going back to Birmingham.

I phoned Bankham social services and asked if they had a contact number for Berkley-Grey. The person I spoke to naturally asked me why I wanted her number, so I explained.

"Hold on," she said. There was a silence for about a minute, and when the woman came back on the line she told me there was no one working there with that name.

I said, "I heard recently she's moved back to Birmingham. All I want is a contact number."

The woman said she did not have one and she could not help me.

I called Birmingham social services and was put through to the personnel department. I asked if Berkley-Grey was now working for them, but the man on the phone checked their records and said he could find no one by that name. He also said that because it was a double-barrelled name, it would have been easy to locate her on the computer records – if she *had* been working for them.

I was running into blocks at every turn. I decided that at the next child protection conference, I would just ask them about Berkley-Grey's whereabouts.

A couple of weeks later, there was another meeting. I seemed to spend more time at meetings that I did at work. During the meeting, I asked the social worker, Carol Foster, if she could give me a contact number for Jan Berkley-Grey and explained why I wanted it. I never held with lying, so I was simply honest.

Foster tried either to act dumb, or was trying to make me appear dumb, because she said, "I don't know who you're talking about."

There were the usual six to eight people at

the meeting, so I said, "Carol, Bankham is only a small town, so I don't imagine there are a vast number of children's social workers employed here. This one is black, too. How many black social workers have there ever been in Bankham?" I questioned her, very sarcastically adding, "Is it possible she's been sent to the moon, for reporting that she could see nothing wrong with my family?"

At this point, the chairperson, Sandra Watkins, butted in and said that "Jan Berkley-Grey was only a trainee social worker, so she wouldn't be qualified to make a report."

"Glad to know she exists, at least," I sighed.

I didn't think fast enough at the time, but in hindsight, I should have asked why, if Jan was only a trainee social worker and not qualified to make a report, was she assigned to the case and working without supervision? What was she doing coming to the house alone, and why were appointments being made for her to work with Sally at school to work on her "life story"?

The real reason I believe that Jan Berkley-Grey was taken off the case and made to "disappear" is because she disagreed with the social workers already involved with the family.

About a week or so later, we were at yet

another meeting at the local family centre. The usual things were being said: they were trying to convince us that we had inadequacies as parents, and I was making it quite clear from my manner that I viewed them as incompetent, corrupt buffoons.

It was getting close to the end of the meeting and it was evident that the people there were eager to leave and get home, so I thought I would tackle Carol Foster about the children's case.

"How long does it normally take for social services to get a care order on children?" I asked Foster.

She replied that they could usually get a care order within a month.

Tapping my head mockingly, I said, "It's taken you over twelve months, so far, with my family. Doesn't that tell you that you've got something wrong?"

"No," Foster replied. "It just tells me that you are very clever."

I could have taken that as a compliment, but it was typical social worker mentality: they cannot accept that *they* can make mistakes and that *they* can get things wrong. And this is what makes them very dangerous to a family, and especially to

153

children. Once a decision has been made early in a case, they seem unable or unwilling to change or modify their views.

I then asked Foster again, "Can you tell me where Jan Berkley-Grey is now?"

Foster pinched the bridge of her nose with her fingers, her eyes closed as if in pain. "Why do you keep trying to find *her*?"

"I feel it would be good to get her involved," I said, "because she had a totally different view about the family. This should be enough, in itself, to get you to examine your immovable attitudes and opinions. Give you a more balanced view."

"You will never be allowed to contact Jan Berkley-Grey," Foster told me.

This reply came as a bit of a shock, so I decided to try a different tactic. Controversial, but I was hopeful that it would push her to tell me where Berkley-Grey was. So, I asked, "Did you get rid of her because she's black?"

"No," her instant response came. "You won't be allowed to contact Jan because if you did – it might help your case."

An icy cold wave of shock came over me, as the meaning of her reply sank in. I recall saying to Foster, "I thought this was about finding out if there actually *is* a problem with the children within the family? Not about who can get the best case together, and who can block the other's evidence?"

The expression on Foster's face made it obvious that she wished she hadn't let this reply slip out.

After I left the meeting and thought some more about Foster's reply, it all became clear to me. *If social services carry out a child protection investigation, but only allow people to be involved if they are prepared to collude in their negative view about the family... and they deliberately exclude professionals who disagree with them... then the investigation has been deliberately corrupted! These so-called child protection workers are not working in the best interests of the children or family at all! They have such an attitude of superiority and conviction that the first decision they make is the right one, they will not change their position and are not able to see common sense!*

I thought the time would soon come when social services would get a court date for the application for a full care order on Sally. It seemed that they were giving priority to Sally's case first, above our other children's, presumably because of the previous case involving her, some years before. I think they saw Sally as the weak link: the first easy target, and once they got a care order on Sally, that would make it easier for them to make a case to remove Rachel and John, as well.

Since they had got a psychiatrist and a psychologist of their own choosing to give reports on Sally, I asked my solicitor, "Why can't I have an independent child psychiatrist, to make a report for us?"

My solicitor replied that I had the legal right to this, if it was an option that I wanted to take.

Thanks for not telling me before! I thought. *You would have thought the solicitor acting for you would be making all the best recommendations – and actually trying to help you! But no, they seem to do the bare legal minimum that is required of them!*

Actually, on one occasion, after I had informed the solicitor about one of the many written complaints I had made to social services, my solicitor actually remarked to me, "I can see why social services hate you so much! You scrutinise every report they make – and you pull them up on every little detail."

I frowned, slightly stung by this. *Of course, I would!* I didn't say anything to her, but I thought, *Maybe you would scrutinise their reports if it were your children they were trying to take!*

We found an independent child psychiatrist, Dr Al-Cadeen, who said he would assess Sally. My solicitor informed social services that we were exercising our right to have our own assessment carried out and they agreed to it. But they said that, due to Sally's frail emotional state, they could not allow Dr Al-Cadeen to see Sally in person, because in their opinion, this would cause Sally more damage! Instead, he would only be allowed access to the reports that had already been made on her, and they said he could make his assessment based on those! My blood ran cold, at the thought that he would only have their biased reports and negative views to go on, rather than talking to Sally himself and making his own opinion.

I complained to my solicitor, saying, "They can't do this, can they?"

My solicitor said that, apparently, they could. She reckoned that as long as they gave our psychiatrist access to paper assessments, social services had met their legal obligations.

How devious they seemed to be! They were

fully prepared for Sally to be assessed in person as many times as they needed it to happen until they got the result they wanted – and then, suddenly she was too fragile to be assessed in person by our expert!

Dr Al-Cadeen was given the reports concerning Sally. Due to him having access to the reports from the school, the speech and language therapist, and various other parties concerning the two younger children – documenting that they were normal and not affected by our parenting – his conclusion was that any problem there might be concerning Sally was likely to be of a genetic nature, rather than caused by parenting. It was the best we could achieve, under the circumstances.

The full care order court hearing took place in **January 1997**. My solicitor and I met with our barrister in Woodshire Crown Court. The barrister told us that we were to go before a very senior judge who had a reputation for being harsh with people. She was a little breathless as she told us, and she warned me that the judge might say some very unpleasant things to me – or speak to me in a way that I might find frightening. I blinked at her, looking blankly into her wide, alarmed eyes. She said it was not too late to back down and the court could deal with the case without us.

"No," I insisted. "I'll go into court. The judge can't call me anything that I haven't already been called."

She licked her lips nervously, and I noticed a film of sweat on her face. It seemed that this young barrister was frightened, herself, of going before this judge.

I was convinced that, once we were in court and the evidence was heard – Sally's school reports up until she entered Mrs Bell's class and the reports after she had left Mrs Bell's class, and Dr Al-Cadeen's report – it would be clear-cut. What had I got to worry about? Surely the application for a care order would be refused!

We went into court and were before Judge Robert Martin. The court was informed by the local authority's barrister that Mrs Bell, the teacher, had telephoned earlier that morning to say she had taken ill and was not able to attend. My hopes rose.

If I remember correctly, the first person to take to the witness box was Kathleen Archer from child protection.

The judge said, "Ms Archer – I spent a degree of time reading over the paperwork last evening, and there are a couple of things I noticed in the social services report, which I want to query."

Kathleen Archer nodded briskly, her eyes wide.

He said, "There appears to be no indication of how this family came to the attention of social services. Ms Archer, can you give any clarification on this?"

"Ummm... Er..." Archer began to mumble. She did not have an answer.

I stifled a smile. *Aha! You've been caught out by a sharp judge – and now you're for it!* I thought to myself.

Judge Martin could see she had no answer and pressed on: "Was it concerns from other professional bodies that got you involved with the family?"

"Yes. Yes!" Archer replied, gratefully.

"I thought that must have been the case," said the judge, smugly.

I was in utter bewilderment. What had just happened?

Judge Martin then mentioned Archer's comment about me in her statement. "You say Mr Jordan presented as a – and I quote - 'paranoid' person."

This was a gem! *You can't just say that about someone! That's an actual clinical diagnosis!* Surely the judge would have something to say about Archer making a mental health assessment of me – when she had, at least to *my* knowledge, no mental health training?

I was wrong. Judge Martin said, "I looked in the dictionary last evening and one of the definitions of paranoia was 'having a very different view to yourself that you find to be unreasonable'. Is that so, Ms Archer?"

What? What the hell?

"Mmm... yes." Archer nodded.

"Then I accept your comment, based on this dictionary definition."

I gave an audible gasp. My interpretation of what had just been said by Judge Martin was that if you disagreed with social services, they could actually state that you have a certifiable mental health problem, simply because you disagreed with them! More worryingly, it seemed that the courts would accept this!

I broke into a sweat, feeling sick. I was rapidly coming to the conclusion that I should have just gone home and let the court come to their predetermined decision.

But we still had our expert, Dr Al-Cadeen. Into the witness box he went, but when asked by our barrister for his assessment, he said he had no option but to agree with social services' assessment!

What? That came a little out of the blue, to say the least!

Our barrister asked why he had suddenly changed his view from his original assessment.

He informed the court, "After being asked to attend a meeting called by the guardian ad litem, Patricia Hughes, a couple of days ago…"

What? I almost cried out. *They've nobbled my expert!*

"… and listening to their opinion that Sally has made significant improvement since being with foster parents, I had no option but to agree with them."

I swallowed down a throatful of bile that had risen with my fear.

He ended, "Yes, Sally's problem could still be of a genetic origin. Only time will tell."

I was raging inside, but trying to contain myself. If Dr Al-Cadeen was our expert witness, then how on earth were social workers allowed to have meetings with him, without our knowledge?

Psychiatrist Dr Tracy Swinton then entered the witness box and was asked by our barrister about Sally's supposed improvement after she had been placed in voluntary care.

Dr Swinton said she was aware of these improvements.

Our barrister asked her if she was also aware of any improvements in Sally *before* she went into care, and Dr Swinton confirmed that she was.

Our barrister said, "I put it to you, Dr Swinton, that if reports showed that Sally was improving after leaving Oldenhurst First School, before she went into care, then surely any improvement was not due to being with foster parents, but was merely a continuation of the improvements recorded while she was still at home!"

"No," Dr Swinton denied that was the case and stated that, "If Sally had not been removed from the home, she would have stopped improving."

I felt like shouting out. Why wasn't anyone asking what Sally was supposed to be improving from? Her school reports showed a bubbly, talkative child – until she entered Mrs Bell's class. Mrs Bell had made the statement telling how damaged Sally was… but Sally said she was frightened of Mrs Bell because she had shaken her violently in front of the whole class, hurting her arms!

Once Sally had left Mrs Bell's class and gone to middle school, the reports there documented a bubbly, talkative child again!

Oldenhurst First School had put it in writing that social services had said that the school was not to talk to Sally about the alleged assault, because of the harm it would do to her. Why did social services want the assault covered up?

Dr Swinton was then asked, "Why, if Sally was so badly damaged, did the foster parents say, in psychologist Kelly Andrews' report, that they have never seen the damaged child that everyone is describing? From the moment Sally came to stay with them, she has always been a happy girl."

Dr Swinton said, "Sally's normal behaviour was unusual."

"Why so?" our barrister enquired.

Now try and get your head around this next exchange, if you can. The only reason she could give for this 'unusual' behaviour was that Sally had been in care as a baby from the age of eight weeks to the age of three years. Although during this time, she had learnt the ability to relate to others.

"When Sally was returned to her birth parents, she lost this ability," Dr Swinton claimed. "But regained it in foster care."

When she came into contact with the present foster parents, she subconsciously and instantly recovered it again?

How could you possibly deal with twisted logic like this? If it was not so scary, it would be funny!

These were so-called experts, spouting supposed logic that could never realistically be described as such – and the judge was lapping it up! No mention was made of the fact that while Sally was with foster parents as a baby, I was visiting almost every day, caring for her, bathing her and taking her out in her pushchair. They conveniently forgot about this.

I watched helplessly, as it all played out before me. Needless to say, my initial optimism was wrong. They got the care order.

It was only some time later, after writing complaint after complaint to the local authority, asking why no one would talk to Sally about the assault by her teacher, that I found out the reason. Kathleen Archer had informed all concerned that for

Sally to be interviewed about her teacher's alleged assault would be considered – by Archer – to be an act of abuse in itself.

What sort of power do social services have, when they can say that anyone attempting to investigate an allegation will, themselves, be accused of child abuse? I think Martha's psychiatric nurse, Sharon Fowler, hit the nail on the head when she said that the social workers were acting as if it were a medieval witch-hunt.

To add insult to injury, within a few weeks of the full care order being granted, we were informed that social services would be moving Sally to a different school!

I complained to Kathleen Archer. "You told me, even before the voluntary care order was made, that it was important to keep Sally at the same school! So Sally's life would remain as stable as possible!"

"Things change," Archer said. "It's more convenient for her foster parents if she moves schools."

So much for keeping Sally's life as normal as possible.

Chapter 11

Now that they had the care order on Sally, they could increase their efforts to get care orders on Rachel and John – presumably on the grounds that if our parenting had caused such damage to Sally, then surely the two younger children must be at equal risk? But social services had not bargained for the fact that I had learnt how well they can twist the meaning behind every situation, by this time.

A great example, previously mentioned, was their assertion that John's not asking permission to take something from the fridge showed a lack of boundaries, but that Rachel, who *had* asked permission, would not have felt the need to do so, if she felt comfortable in her home environment.

By now, I was using their own methods against them. Time was moving on, and I went to meeting after meeting with social services and the family centre staff. My tactics were preventing them from compiling any grounds to go to court to take the two younger children. They would try to fabricate evidence, and every time, I would pull it apart.

I attended every meeting that involved my

family because I knew that if I wasn't there, they would put whatever they wanted into the reports. You'd have thought they'd have kept the timetable of these meetings from me, to prevent me from attending – because I can tell you, they did *not* like me being there at all! But I had made it very clear that I wanted to be informed of every meeting.

Kathleen Archer once said to me, "David, there's a meeting due soon, but there's no need for you to attend."

I said to Archer, "I want to be informed about *every* meeting that involves my family. And if, for whatever reason, I am not informed about a meeting and because of that, I do not attend, I will *not* accept anything that's been said or reported at any such meeting – on the grounds of my not being present."

I would have been denied the right to my opinion or views being heard and the opportunity to defend myself from any accusations. As far as I was concerned, this would be a violation of my human rights. I used this "violation of human rights" term against them several times. I knew that whenever I used this term, they hated it; it really wound them up.

Just like before, they wouldn't give me a

copy of the minutes of meetings I attended until weeks or even months later, when it was far too late to challenge anything that had been said or written.

On one occasion, in **autumn 1996**, Kathleen Archer called to tell me another meeting was being held at Bankham Town Hall and that because it was only loosely connected to my family case, social workers would not attend; so there was no real need for me to attend, either. I thanked Archer for informing me and I said that if the meeting had the slightest connection with my family, I would be there.

At the town hall meeting, there were many faces I hadn't seen before. It turned out that many of the people present were town councillors who had no interest in what was happening with my family. The main reason for this meeting was to discuss the significant costs that were being incurred by the local authority in dealing with our case.

As previously mentioned, the social worker, Carol Foster, had told me that they could usually get a care order in under a month, but our case had gone on for well over a year. Every week, we were going to the family centre – often the only family there – and this centre had to be staffed by about four people. And they cooked meals for us. The staff would often take us out on a day trip and feed us while we were out, too. Consider that all this had to be paid for by the local authority, and you can start to appreciate the costs that were being incurred. Not to mention the legal costs and all the meetings attended – where there could be up to twelve people present! It all had to be paid for.

One councillor said, "I understand this case is costing the council a lot of money."

Another, who I believe may have been the treasurer, replied, "It has cost the local authority an unbelievable amount of money! We cannot justify spending such an amount on one case."

Another person insisted, "This case had to be brought to a conclusion, and quickly."

To be honest, I cannot recall seeing a single social worker there. I imagine they were probably keeping their heads down. I kept mine down, too – although I felt like saying, *Yes! Tell them to drop it, and let us get on with our lives! Give us our daughter back and leave us alone!*

Shortly after the meeting at the town hall, I received a message saying that Andrew Peterson,

Unit Manager (Child Protection and Planning Review), wished to have a meeting with me in connection with a complaint of mine that had not yet been resolved.

If you recall, a month or so earlier, I had made a written complaint about the child protection review conference chaired by Sandra Watkins, when Linda Berry, the children's charity family centre worker, had submitted a report stating that she had serious concerns about Martha's and my parenting ability. When I asked for these concerns to be made clear to me, Berry said that the problem we had was that we would not accept that we had problems. Watkins said I was not to discuss the matter any further at the meeting and that if I wanted to clarify any concerns with Berry, I should do so later, at the family centre. Watkins indicated that if I continued to press the matter then I would be asked to leave the room and would be reported as having become uncooperative.

I wrote a complaint about Linda Berry writing a report for the court stating that we had problems, yet Sandra Watkins refusing to allow me to establish what the concerns were, which prevented us from being able to defend ourselves against the allegations. And as far as I was concerned, this was a violation of our human rights.

The time of the meeting with Andrew Peterson came – I think it was mid-**December 1996** – at the social services offices in Bankham. Peterson arrived with a colleague, who I believe was Stanley Waltham. Peterson appeared to be the older of the two. He was a relaxed, confident person who was sure of himself, but Waltham seemed even more arrogant and cocky.

We began the meeting, which I had been told was to discuss my "violation of human rights" complaint, and straight away, Peterson began talking about problems with the two younger children!

Now, since Peterson had never seen the children, I couldn't understand why he wanted to talk about them.

"I'm not here to discuss them," I persisted. "You invited me here in relation to my complaint.

"In relation to that, we are concerned about your children, Rachel and John. I'd like to..."

"Just a minute!" I interrupted, again. I pointed out that we were there to discuss my complaint concerning Sandra Watkins and the child protection conference of 7 October 1996.

Stanley Waltham shifted his papers in

agitation. He was sweating and red-faced, biting his lip to prevent himself from snapping at me.

Each time I tried to get on to the subject of my complaint, Peterson or Waltham would change the topic back to problems with the other children! Had it been a social worker or a family centre worker at a child protection conference who was wanting to discuss such problems, then fair enough; but this was a meeting about my complaint (or so I thought)! Why were they both trying to get me to talk about the children?

Something just didn't feel right. It felt as if they were not there to deal with my complaint at all. I employed the broken record technique – consistently drawing them back to the reason I'd been invited to this meeting: my complaint. I could see from Stanley Waltham's manner that he was getting more than a little annoyed that they could not draw me away from the complaint issue. But still, they tried to ignore me, and kept bringing up problems about my children.

Eventually, I had to say to them, "As far as I'm concerned, this meeting was arranged to discuss my complaint! Why do you keep avoiding the issue? Since you apparently only want to talk about the two younger children and you're

173

evidently unwilling to discuss my complaint, you are wasting my time." I started packing up my papers. "We should end this meeting, since it's not achieving anything."

"Who the fucking hell do you think you are?" Waltham shouted, his eyes blazing, and his face purple with rage. "Do you think you are better than us? We have to deal with scum like you every day of the week!"

I must have pushed the right button. I maintained an emotionless expression while Waltham let out this tirade. Andrew Peterson, however, had a look of total shock on his face.

I believe his rage was because I had reversed the roles. I spoke to them in a coolly professional way, as they should have talked to me – and Stanley Waltham responded in a manner in which they could have expected me, a common "service user", to respond!

Peterson took Waltham by the arm and quickly led him out of the room. I could hear them talking animatedly outside for a short time and then Peterson came back in alone, and said, "I must apologise for Stanley. He has had a very stressful day."

We shook hands and left the room. Stanley

Waltham was nowhere in sight. It was obvious that he had felt that I was talking down to them and this had made him lose control.

Can you imagine how he must have felt? He was a senior member of social services and I was a mere service user, who as far as they were concerned, needed to be instructed – by them – in how to live a useful and normal life. And yet, he felt that *I* was talking down to *them*!

His abusive comments do make you realise what some social workers actually think of service users. I can imagine they are probably justified in holding such views, in many cases... But until they can begin to employ some common sense within their training, they are always likely to make avoidable mistakes. They should appreciate that they are fallible, and admit when they are wrong, rather than closing ranks and entrenching themselves – even lying or concealing the truth if it conflicts with their assumptions. Their collective arrogance and disdain was epitomised by Stanley Waltham's outburst. And it will always be some poor person or family that has to suffer the consequences.

I was soon to find out what the real purpose of the meeting had been.

A week or two later, I received a report from social services – and with it, was a statement made by Andrew Peterson.

I read it, with curiosity, and then with increasing concern. He supported social services' views about how severely delayed the children were and the serious damage being caused to them by bad parenting! *What? What did he know?*

And he said that he supported social services request for a care order! I felt sick. He stated that he could find no grounds to believe that I had been denied the right to know what social services' concerns were, but that every effort had been made to highlight their concerns!

This report was like a punch to the stomach, to me. I had been fending off ordinary social workers for a long time, but this was a report from someone in a senior position – someone of authority, whose words had significant impact. And as anyone who has been through the courts will know, the more senior or qualified a witness you can get to support your opinion, the more likely it is that the court will accept your view.

The words swam before my eyes, and it felt as if the world was closing in on me. This report did actually put me in a daze, because for a few moments, I had the real feeling that I had lost. That it was hopeless. Now that social services had this statement from someone in such a senior position, it would be only a short time before they went to court seeking a care order. I could do nothing. I couldn't even think.

But that was only temporary.

Earlier, I said that I had begun to learn how social workers think – and understand how they twist meanings to suit their ends. Now, without realising it, and while I was still in a daze after reading Peterson's report, I must have gone into "social worker mode".

Because, like a bolt out of the blue, it hit me.

"Ah! I've got you, you bastard!" I cried.

I am not the sort of person who swears, if at all possible, so I am not sure that I actually said those words out loud, but it matters not. It was a very strange feeling, indeed.

Subconsciously, I had found something – and a feeling of excitement came over me. It was playing at the fringes of my memory, and I knew I had to grasp it, bring it into my full awareness, grab it and run with it. It was all I had. What was it?

It gradually became clear to me as I recalled

something Martha's psychiatrist once said: "Your family is in the system. Go with the system, because if you try and fight the system, you will lose."

Yes, I agree. If you try to fight the system, you will, more than likely, lose. But... the thought formalised in my mind, becoming more solid and certain... What if you fight just one individual within the system? And who better to target than a person in a senior position within the system?

I grabbed a pen and paper and quickly wrote down what came into my head. It was a letter of complaint addressed to the local authority, and it went along these lines:

I would like to make a complaint about Mr Andrew Peterson. He has written a report supporting social workers' views about damage that has been done to my children due to bad parenting. He supports their views that my children are developmentally delayed in every aspect and that they have behavioural problems, and says that, due to the fact that we do not accept that our bad parenting is causing damage to them, the damage will continue.

The social workers involved with my children are not qualified speech and language therapists; nor are they experts in child behaviour. The social workers' assessments contradict the views of qualified experts, such as the speech and language therapist who assessed the two younger children and reported that they are actually advanced for their ages. The school have said that they have seen no problem with the two younger children and that they are normal and happy.

Martha and I, as the parents of these children, agree completely with the views of the qualified experts and disagree completely with the non-qualified social workers. For Mr Andrew Peterson and the social workers to contradict the qualified professionals and continually refer to my children as being developmentally delayed due to bad parenting will have a detrimental effect on their development — and this constitutes child abuse.

Based on the above information, I would like to make an official complaint against Mr Andrew Peterson for **child abuse.**

Not only was I writing letters of complaint to the local authority, but I had also sent a letter to the local government ombudsman, stating that my human rights had been violated at the child protection conference held on 7 October 1996.

I had written to the ombudsman on several other occasions, in connection with other complaints I had made about the local authority (social services, in particular) but I had found that the ombudsman always seemed to take the same view as the local authority. Therefore, I didn't hold out any hope of a favourable decision on this complaint. Still, I would try anything.

Some time later, the ombudsman had evidently been in contact with the local authority about my complaints of human rights violations and sent me a copy of a letter they had received from the local authority. The letter was dated **14 April 1997**.

It stated that Mr Peterson had investigated my complaint about the meeting and their prevention of disclosing details of our bad parenting – and he was satisfied that there was no substance to my claims. *Hmmm,* I thought. *Typical.*

The letter also stated that Mr Peterson should have informed me that I had further rights to challenge their decision and that Mr Peterson's decision was not the end of the matter as he had made it seem. My eyes widened. This was something new!

The local authority apologised to the ombudsman for what they referred to as 'an oversight'! The letter also asked if the ombudsman would like the local authority to carry out the final stage of the complaint process – the final stage that the local authority had overlooked.

The letter also stated the actual concerns – at last! – that the professionals had, for the welfare of the children – and a copy of all their concerns was printed on the back of the letter, for the ombudsman to see!

This is how the concerns were listed on the

letter:

Current Areas of Concern:

- David minimises professionals' concerns about the children.
- Martha is unable to be assertive enough to share her views or to challenge David.
- David and Martha distort the facts of previous and present events.
- David has refused to accept responsibility for his part in the significant harm of these children. He places responsibility with Martha, Sally, and the professionals.
- David has been blocking Social Workers' involvement and not working with Social Services.
- Sally's presentation, which indicates emotional harm.
- Sally's isolation and scapegoating within the family.
- Sally has no understanding of the situation and the reason for professionals' involvement. This is partly due to the fact that we have been prevented from working with her.
- Parents' lack of management of the children.
- David does not support Martha to overcome her difficulties with the children.
- Rachel seems dominant in the family.
- Rachel's aggression towards Sally and John.

- Rachel's changed behaviour at the family centre.
- John's speech is unclear – language development is not appropriate to his age.
- John is unable to engage in imaginative play or sustain play alone.

If such a list – of 15 items – were handed to anyone, I am sure whoever read it would have serious concerns about the welfare of the children, taken on face value. This is exactly what social services wanted. But if you look carefully at the list, are they what most people would consider to be real, serious problems? Or are they what could be seen as just "social-worker speak" – when social workers use waffle to imply that there's a problem in a situation that is normal?

Let us look at Martha, to begin with. She was under psychiatric care and was heavily medicated, so was hardly able to assert herself – as the social workers mentioned, in the list. With regard to Rachel and John, they were, by now, in full-time education and the school were aware of the position the family was in. The school had no concerns – and both Rachel and John had been assessed by a child speech and language therapist who was recommended by our family doctor. She had said that both Rachel and John were actually advanced for their age, contrary to the social workers' assertion that John's speech was unclear and underdeveloped for his age. Social services were in contact with the schools, so why were they totally ignoring their school or, as in the past, twisting facts?

In the list, Sally is portrayed as a very damaged child. But why is there no mention of her assault accusation against her teacher? And no reference to social services telling the school that under no circumstances was Sally to be interviewed about the assault? They said this decree was due to Sally's frail emotional state, and any enquiry would, in itself, be an abuse! And yet, Social services seemed to have forgotten that Sally was emotionally strong enough for them to allow her to be accessed by a psychiatrist and a psychologist, when it suited them.

I had contacted the ombudsman asking him to look into my allegation that my human rights had been violated. Due to the fact that the local authority had not completed the full complaints process, it would seem logical that the ombudsman would need to wait until the full complaints process had been carried out before he could look into it. I was not shown copies of any further correspondence between the ombudsman and the local authority. And the final stage of my complaint process was never carried out, because just days after receiving the letter from the ombudsman, dated **14 April 1997**, I was informed that another child protection meeting had been arranged for **24 April 1997**. There were just ten days between the two dates. Someone was moving fast.

Chapter 12

I think things must have begun to feel very messy for the local authority, now that the ombudsman had become involved. Remember that these child-care cases are renowned for their secrecy, but with the ombudsman waiting for the final outcome of my complaint, the local authority must have been in a quandary over what to do next.

I think my latest complaint about Andrew Peterson and the social workers' actions constituting child abuse against my children must have just about worked its way through the system, by that point. I was accusing the local authority not only of violation of human rights but also child abuse. I bet this does not happen to them very often. Especially from someone they have come to detest so much: the "Mega Pig".

Martha and I attended the child protection meeting, as we always did. Since these meetings were during the working day, everyone I knew was at work – or did not want to be seen as involved. This, I can fully understand; because for many people, the mere mention of social services provokes fear and dread. What a terrible thing it is when the very organisation that is meant to look after the well-being of children and families terrifies them to such an extent! So, each time we attended a meeting – and there were many, I can tell you – we would arrange for the children to be looked after at the family centre.

The meeting was chaired, as usual, by Sandra Watkins. I was preparing for Andrew Peterson's statement about the children to be used against us. The complaint I had made about his actions constituting child abuse was to try to counter his statement; but from experience, I knew that social services would just ignore what was not to their liking, so I really did not know what to expect.

Nothing in my wildest dreams could have prepared me for what was about to happen next.

The usual way these meetings proceeded was for the chair to introduce each person present, which Watkins did. The chair would then outline the current concerns about the children and ask for comments. Sally's case was not included in this meeting, since she was now in care.

On this occasion, Watkins said that various reports had come in from professionals, including the school and the child speech and language therapist. I braced myself to challenge yet more biased accounts, as they twisted the evidence.

She went on: "... and all these report that both children have shown great improvement. There now appears to be no concern about Rachel and John's development..."

What? I jerked my head back in surprise, my eyes wide. I was completely taken aback by the comments. This was the first time ever that anyone connected with the local authority had openly mentioned the views of the school that Rachel and John attended – and the assessment made by the speech and language therapist – without twisting the facts. These reports had been available to the local authority for twelve months or more! So, why were they suddenly being referenced now?

Watkins asked if there was anyone at the table who wanted to comment.

The social worker, Carol Foster, said, "Hmmm... I still have serious concerns about the children," she pressed her lips together, a sour look on her face. "And also about Martha's ability to look after herself – due to her being on medication."

Oh, here we go, I thought. *This is where it continues...*

"The reports that had been made available

are from qualified professionals within their field," Watkins said, to my amazement. "And Martha's medication is being administered by mental health professionals. Carol, do you have appropriate qualifications in the field on which your concerns are based?"

I sat, open-mouthed. This was totally unexpected.

She went on: "... Or are your concerns just based on your own opinion?"

Foster glowered and replied that her concerns were her opinion as a "professional social worker".

Watkins said, "We are only interested in facts today, not personal feelings."

"But that's ridiculous!" Foster protested. "I am a...!"

"Be quiet!" Watkins told her.

The look of shock on Foster's face was clear to see. It probably mirrored my own, although mine was tinted with the blossoming of a tiny bud of hope and a flicker of almost... triumph that there were some signs of sense and justice, at last.

Something had clearly gone on behind the scenes – and it was obvious, from her face, that Foster had not been aware of it.

Sandra Watkins was now using terms like "academically qualified professionals" – phrases I had used in my child abuse complaint letter!

Watkins then began a speech, saying, "It is obvious that the local authority's views on how to raise children differ from yours. However, based on the fact that the children are growing and developing – and with no concerns from qualified professionals expressed, then all we can really do is agree to disagree about one another's methods."

She said that she couldn't say that we were wrong and they were right, or that they were wrong and we were right. Only that we just had different methods, with both methods obtaining the same end result: normal, well-balanced children.

What a load of rubbish! I thought to myself. Their methods, our methods... what the hell was she talking about?

We just tried to have a normal family, like everyone else. Except our family had not been allowed to be normal for years – because we had social services scrutinising everything we did – and claiming that everything we did was wrong! I had to keep my lips tightly shut.

After Watkins concluded her speech, she asked for everyone in favour of removing the children's names from the at-risk register to raise their hands. Watkins raised her hand as she spoke and, as normal at these meetings, everyone else followed suit. Except Carol Foster.

Watkins sternly looked over at Foster, who sat with her arms folded, and her jaw set. I think Foster knew, just from that look, that Watkins was telling her to raise her hand.

"I still have concerns," Foster muttered.

Sandra Watkins glared at her, saying, "We will note your concerns."

And so, the decision was made to take the children's names off the at-risk register!

I noticed that, unusually, not a single member of the child protection team was at the meeting. Had they been kept away, or simply not informed about the meeting?

Watkins then asked if there was anything social services could do to help the family, in light of Martha's problems.

"I asked for help from social services at the beginning of our involvement with them," I said. "And we were told the only action they were prepared to take would be to remove the children from the home!"

Watkins said, "Ah, but it would be different

now!"

Frankly, I wasn't willing to take that risk. I wanted to get out of there with our victory – not end up with them shifting their focus to Martha, with the potential for them to find, or fabricate, more 'concerns'.

I told her, "Thank you. Although our family could have done with help because of Martha's condition when I first asked for it, I am not prepared to have any further contact with social services."

So, the meeting ended.

It felt surreal! They had put the children on the at-risk register on 1 August 1995 (after much pressure in the years before) and for all this time, we had been looked down upon by social services as the parents from hell (the "Mega Pig" family)! Even up to 14 April 1997, when the local authority sent the letter to the ombudsman listing all their concerns about us and the children! And then – just ten days later, at this last child protection meeting, suddenly they had no concerns at all and removed the children from the register? What had happened in those ten days? I cannot be certain, but I think the child abuse complaint letter I'd sent in had something to do with it!

The social workers – especially Kathleen Archer and Suzie Ralph from the child protection team – had been so adamant from the start that the children were being abused by their parents! So strong was their determination to remove all the children from the Home, that they had continually ignored or distorted the views of the school and the speech therapist – who, after all, were the professionals best qualified to assess the children.

Does this give you the impression that social services were carrying out a vendetta against the family, because they had taken a dislike to the parents? Social workers had continually claimed that we had deceived them in the past and that we distorted events! Maybe the severe action they had been taking was a punitive response to the deception they perceived me to be displaying. Maybe, to them, removing the children would be payback for me being 'problematic'. I still fumed at the injustice of it all – that they would drag innocent children away from their parents at the least opportunity! It was unconscionable.

It does show that social workers are a law unto themselves, if even the senior management in a local authority cannot openly challenge them. Look at it this way: I send in a serious complaint of child abuse against a senior social worker. The very mention of child abuse – from whatever source, aimed at any target – is a serious allegation. It surely must be taken seriously. Even when the accusation came from me, a person who, by this time, the local authority had marked as a serial complainer!

The basis of my accusation was that qualified professionals were being ignored. I'd been saying this for years, to no avail. Now, imagine senior people from the local authority studying the accusation and finding the details of the accusation to be accurate! Recognising that qualified professionals were being ignored, or their comments distorted – and that, only recently, the local authority had been forced to apologise to the ombudsman in connection with a previous complaint by me! Would they dare allow my latest child abuse complaint to get as far as the ombudsman? I don't think so!

Even when it must have been obvious that social services had gone so far off the tracks, it seemed that the only way for the children to be taken off the at-risk register was for social services to be outmanoeuvred.

I believe this is what happened at the child

protection meeting. Carol Foster seemed to have been taken completely by surprise when the chair told her that the meeting was only interested in opinions from "appropriately qualified professionals".

If Foster was totally unaware that the children's names were going to be removed from the at-risk register at this meeting, then it would stand to reason that Kathleen Archer from the child protection team would also have been totally unaware of what was about to happen.

Out of all the social workers involved with our family, Archer appeared to be the most hostile towards Martha and myself. If Archer had been aware that the intention was to remove the children's names at this meeting, then you would imagine that she and a whole team of social workers and child protection workers would have turned up. And they would almost certainly have voted en masse against the chair's recommendations!

Later that day, after hearing the outcome of the meeting, I imagine there must have been some seriously angry and annoyed social and child protection workers.

Martha and I left the meeting and drove back

to the children's charity family centre, to collect Rachel and John. I was bubbling with excitement, and Martha was smiling in disbelief.

When we arrived there, one of the staff asked how it had gone, as they usually did, after we had been to a meeting.

And I would always reply the same: "The children are still on the register".

The staff would habitually say, "Well, it's for the best".

On this occasion, I was able to say that the children's names had been removed from the register!

The look of shock on the assistant's face was priceless! A few seconds later, she said, "Well, it was obvious there was nothing wrong with the children. So, they did the right thing, removing their names from the register."

I shook my head. *Unbelievable!* It really was enough to make you sick to the stomach. For almost two years, social services and this children's charity had done everything in their power to remove the children. And then, in an instant, they say that there is nothing wrong with the children, or our parenting!

Two weeks later, on **19 May 1997,** I received a letter from Andrew Peterson, the senior social worker I had accused of child abuse, informing us that the children's names had been removed from the register and hoping the action taken by the council had satisfied and resolved my complaint!

He also asked what further steps I would like to see taken, if I was not satisfied.

I replied to say that I was not happy with everything that had gone on, but I basically left it there. Ultimately, all most of us want is a quiet, peaceful life.

But something in my complaints had clearly frightened someone at a high level! Unless it was because they had just become as sick of me as I was of them – but I doubt it.

What had happened to the social services department, that it had become so corrupt that the very people they are there to help are too afraid to ask for help – in case they are not listened to, and their children are taken from them? To me, it seemed that the child protection team were trained to interpret everything in a negative way – and once they had made a decision, they and the social workers became blinkered. Common sense and reasoning went out of the window.

If the school gave such positive reports for Rachel and John, you may be wondering why Sally's school report was so bad. The simple reason is that they were different schools. We put Rachel and John into Granners First School, whereas Sally had attended Oldenhurst First School. The damning statement made by Sally's teacher, Mrs Bell was, in all probability, a means of covering up her assault on Sally. Discrediting Sally, in case of any investigation, and setting hares off in another direction to divert attention from Mrs Bell's actions. But, due to the fact that Kathleen Archer refused to allow anyone to interview Sally or any of her classmates about the assault, we will probably never know, for sure, the full details of what transpired.

With the two younger children now off the at-risk register, I now had to decide what to do about Sally, who was still under a care order and living with foster parents. Should I challenge the care order? If I did, I knew that it would probably take up to a year to get to court. Sally was almost thirteen years old by this time, so she was too old for social services to have her adopted against our wishes. She was only living about two miles away, and there was, by this time, a lot of contact with her. She was being looked after well by the foster parents and she seemed to like it there. So, for the sake of her stability, I decided that I would leave things how they were. I made an appointment to see the solicitor, to say that our involvement with social services had all but ended. This allowed the solicitor to close the case and terminate financial support from the legal aid department.

I did say to the solicitor just before I left her office, "I guess we'll have to keep our heads down, Now, so's not to give social services any reason to come after us again!"

I was a little surprised by her reply: "I don't think social services will come after your family again."

"Why?" I asked.

She said that I had cost the local authority far too much money and they would not want to go through that again.

Chapter 13

It was time to pick up the pieces and move on with our lives. All the children seemed happy; Martha was on medication, so she was as normal as anyone could be in that condition – and life became relatively ordinary.

After all that had gone on, and the appalling way social services had acted towards the family – and towards Martha in particular, I began to think about various aspects of what had happened over the years.

I remembered the GP stating that Martha appeared to be a very level-headed and sensible young woman before giving birth to Sally. I recalled the way Sally had come to be forcibly removed from Martha in the street... That image was seared into my brain. It was the catalyst to these years of distress, and the starting point to so many hours of time and energy, battling to keep my children. And I considered the ways in which social services had told so many lies, and how they had even fabricated evidence against Martha for the purpose of getting Sally adopted. And I remembered that Martha had even finished up in a psychiatric hospital. Desperate times. And she still wasn't well – damaged forever.

I remembered the psychiatrist once telling me that it was widely considered that shock or traumatic experiences in a person's life could possibly trigger the onset of the sort of mental illness from which Martha suffered. The more I thought about it, the more cruel and unjust it seemed. Social services had gone out of their way to destroy our family unit – and in doing so, they had more than likely destroyed Martha's mental health, too. I had been fire-fighting up to that point – trying to fend off social services' attacks. Now that I had some respite from that, we still couldn't live happily ever after. Martha was a shadow of her former self, and we had suffered so much over the years. I came to the conclusion that I wanted to be pro-active in getting some justice for Martha, because she wasn't in a fit state to stand up for herself.

I searched the Yellow Pages for a solicitor who could possibly look into taking legal action against social services, for causing Martha's illness. I considered that I had sufficient documentation to support my claims – but the biggest obstacle would be funding the legal action. I had no money, so if I were to proceed, it would all depend on us being eligible for legal aid.

I found a firm of solicitors in Kidderminster who seemed experienced in this sort of action, and I contacted them. It was early **May 1997** and they agreed to see me, and would also establish if I could claim legal aid. I took with me what I considered to be the relevant documents.

After some discussion, the solicitor said that he thought that I had a good case against the local authority; but it would be up to the legal aid board to decide whether they thought the case was strong enough for them to fund it. If the legal aid board consider that a case is weak, they will not provide support.

The solicitor said, "It would appear that Sally was unlawfully "snatched" by the social worker when she was five weeks old."

In order to pursue a claim that social services' actions had caused Martha's illness, I was told that we would need a report from a psychiatrist. This would need to state that Martha's condition had been brought on by social services' actions – or at least that it was likely, or possible, that this traumatic situation had led to it. Without such a report, the solicitor confirmed, it would not be possible to pursue the claim. I nodded, considering. Since we'd been told this previously, it shouldn't be too hard to get an expert witness to put something to that effect in writing – I hoped.

Within a few days, I was contacted by the solicitor to say that the legal aid board had considered my case and were prepared to fund it… under certain conditions!

"What are they?" I asked, hopefully.

"Come into this office to sign the paperwork," he said. "And I will explain what the legal aid board conditions are."

Of course, I made an appointment for the earliest opportunity.

The first condition was that I should pay a small monthly amount towards the costs. This was not a great amount, and I could afford it, so I agreed. The second condition was that the legal aid board wanted to be informed of every stage of action that was taken. Their reason was that they had previously fully funded my child protection case against social services. By law, when it comes to children, the costs are fully met by legal aid.

My solicitor told me that the legal aid board had noted that the cost of funding me in the child protection case had gone into five figures. For what appeared to be a straightforward case, this sort of sum was unprecedented. This made me remember what my previous solicitor had remarked on, after the child care case had finished: that she felt social services would not pursue us again because we had already cost them far too much money.

When you think that the legal aid you receive is really the bare minimum required... For our family, that was well into five figures, but what on earth had it cost the local authority, with their top legal team? And their funding the children's charity with a full team of staff to cater for us and all the related costs, to oversee our children and hold regular meetings? I can see why the local authority had that council meeting at the town hall to discuss how much our case was costing them – and also, I can see why they had brought the case to an abrupt end!

So, keeping legal aid fully informed was no problem, and perfectly reasonable, as far as I was concerned.

Our solicitor began to put a case together, writing letters to the local authority, stating our case against them. Meanwhile, I contacted Martha's psychiatrist, to ask if he would be prepared to write a letter to the effect that Martha's mental illness could have been the result of social services' actions, in his professional opinion.

At first, he was very reluctant, saying, "Well, it's difficult to know for sure! And it *is* possible that some other trauma could have been responsible."

However, when I mentioned that my solicitor had said that we would need the support of a mental health specialist to pursue a case against social services, his attitude changed, and he became more supportive.

"If you have a solicitor who thinks that you have a good case," he said, "and they are prepared to take it on, then I will consider writing a report, on what I think could be the cause of Martha's illness."

I breathed a sigh of relief.

"However, I will need to see written confirmation that a solicitor is pursuing the case."

"Absolutely," I said, my hopes rising.

In the meantime, I set about trying to find the names of the magistrates who had rejected the child abuse allegations in **1986**. For a magistrate to come to the judgment she did then, I was certain that she would surely remember the details of the case, and why the care order had been presented.

I contacted Bankham Magistrates Court, explained what I was looking for and why, and I was put in touch with a person responsible for court records. I was told that it could take several days, so I was advised to call back in about a week's time.

I left it a week and called back, but the news was not good. I was told that child protection laws had been updated and records were now being kept on file for years, but unfortunately, this change took place after **1986**. They said that because of the time that had passed, and due to the type of case it was, no minutes of the court hearing were kept on file, from that time.

This avenue of investigation had come to a dead end, so I decided that the next avenue to pursue for information would be to contact the guardian ad litem who had been present in court in **1986,** when the magistrates dismissed the charges of assault against Martha. She would surely remember the events of that day, but how was I to find her? This was before the days of quick and easy searches on the Internet. I knew her name and I knew that she was a social worker from Gloucestershire, but that was all I knew. I phoned Gloucester social services to see if I could locate her, but the only information they would give me was that she had retired some years earlier.

I concluded that the only possible way of locating her was with the use of the good old telephone directory. That was, of course, if she was listed, because many people in her field tend to be ex-directory. I went to the local library to look at the telephone directory for Gloucestershire, writing down the numbers of all the people with the same surname and then I went back to my place of work to start phoning them all, in the hope of finding the right person.

No such luck. So, I went back to the library and the phone books. They had directories that covered the whole country, so I worked my way outwards from Gloucestershire, writing down the numbers from four directories at a time, before going back to work to try them.

I had to keep in mind that it was quite possible that even if I found the right number, someone else, such as her husband, could answer. I had to be prepared to explain myself and who I was trying to find with each call that I made. After several weeks of trawling the phone books, I finally called a number in the south of the country.

A gentleman answered and after me

explaining about the person I was trying to find and the reason for my search, the gentleman said, "It's my wife you are looking for, but she is out at the moment. Could you call back later?"

What a feeling of excitement to have located the guardian! But the excitement would be short-lived.

I called back and spoke to the woman, recounting the details of what had happened in the court all those years ago, to refresh her memory of who I was.

"I wonder – could you give me any information from your recollections of the court case and the reason for the care order being granted?" I asked.

But she merely confirmed that she had been the guardian and told me she was not allowed to discuss any details of the case with me. "I will now have to contact Gloucester social services – because you have made contact with me," she said. "It's for them to decide if any information were to be made available to you from the notes I made. That is, if they still exist."

Any information, it seemed, would have to come from them. She was no help at all.

It did, however, make me think about that

day in court, when the magistrate became visibly angry and said she could not accept social services' case.

Since the case was being thrown out, Martha and I could have immediately gone and collected Sally from the foster parents.

The guardian's quick response was that because of the baby's young age, mother and daughter should be reunited as soon as possible. However, she said also that Martha should not be allowed to take Sally back to the current property and Bankham social services should find Martha suitable accommodation as soon as possible. Was that intended to help Martha, or just a very good way to deceive the magistrates into allowing a custody order to be granted?

No matter what the reason was, as soon as everyone left the court, social services had the care order and they could then do as they pleased. Which was made very clear to me when I asked Sharon Daily about finding Martha some accommodation – and she referred to the magistrates as "silly old women," told me they wouldn't help, and that Martha would never have the baby back!

This guardian was a seasoned social worker

from a different area, but she would have been to court many times, representing the child's best interests, so she would have known how the system worked and how to manage it when it did not work for them. Had the guardian been duped by the Bankham social workers, or had she been extremely clever and outwitted the magistrates?

The guardian who was involved with us ten years later, in **1996,** claimed to be impartial, but she had told me that if I did not agree with social services, then she would have to side with them! Could this really be described as her being impartial? It seemed that the message was: "Do as you are told, or we will slap you down".

Realising that help from the first guardian was a non-starter, I went back to the solicitor, who launched into a series of correspondence.

Chapter 14

After some days, the solicitor began to receive replies to the letters he had sent to the local authority. At first, I was optimistic, but as more and more letters were being exchanged between the solicitor and the local authority, I began to have my doubts about the solicitor's capabilities in handling the case. The local authority seemed to be running rings around him. And in addition, the reply from a specialist barrister my solicitor had contacted regarding our chances of success, came back negative. The odds were against us.

I lost faith and began to realise that the solicitor was completely out of his depth. The local authority was almost ridiculing him. The first allegation we made against the local authority was about Sally's forcible removal, which our solicitor quite rightly referred to as "unlawful snatching". Social Services' response to this was: "Obviously, child law is not an area of law you are familiar with."

They simply stated that Martha's mental health issues weren't caused by Sally's removal – in fact, according to them, Martha was already suffering from mental illness and they claimed that this was the reason Martha had inflicted such serious injuries on the child. That's why Sally had been removed under a Place of Safety order – which they said had been issued *after* a doctor's report noted severe injuries in Sally.

There was clearly a huge hole in their claim!

How did a doctor get to examine Sally *before* she was taken by the social workers? It was the social workers who took her to the doctor! Sally had already been removed from her mother *before* a Place of Safety order had even been applied for. And before a doctor had seen her. Clearly their assertion was not true. And this was all without mentioning the fact that there had been no proof of any injuries! No doctor's report – except for their claims, based on hearsay!

Social Services had twisted things to suit their required version of events and clearly, it was totally outside the capability of this solicitor to deal with it.

From my past experience of legal aid solicitors and from knowing how totally inadequate they can be when it comes to taking on a local authority's legal team, I decided that I needed a different solicitor. More pertinently, a *better* solicitor. However, it's difficult to know who is a good one, because you can only tell how good they are when you see them in action, up against other solicitors. The legal aid board don't like you chopping and changing, and if you mess them around, you can find your financial support withdrawn. If I changed my solicitor this once, I needed to be sure I had a great solicitor next time, because I would have to commit to them – or lose everything. I needed someone brilliant.

Forget local solicitors, I thought to myself, *where do the top people in any profession work?*

London, of course! And the best of the best work in central London – the Square Mile. That was my thinking, anyway.

By now, I had access to the Internet, so I began looking for solicitors based in central London who might be interested in my case. They would also have to be prepared to work for legal aid, because my pockets were empty.

At last, I found a company that looked promising; so, in **September 1998,** I sent them an email giving them a rough outline of my case and asked them if they would consider looking at it.

They replied, asking me to phone them to talk about the case. My hopes rose.

I spoke to them for some time, explaining my version of events, and the happy outcome was that they said they would be prepared to look into my claim, but the legal aid funding would need to be transferred to them.

"Of course!" I said, excited that we might actually be getting somewhere. "That only seems reasonable."

"Right," they said. "We will inform your previous solicitor about what is happening and instruct them to transfer the legal aid. We will also request them to send over all the documentation you have supplied to them."

I put the phone down, my heart beating fast, with gratitude and anticipation.

"Things are looking up," I told Martha, unable to contain my optimism.

"You really think so?" she said, with a watery smile. She knew better than to get her hopes up, after so many disappointments. And she was right.

Over the next month, I received several letters from the solicitor in London saying that he was having difficulty getting the paperwork from my previous solicitors, who seemed reluctant to hand the papers over.

On **10 November 1998,** the London solicitor

sent me a copy of a letter they had sent to my previous solicitor, saying that if the files were not made available forthwith, it might be necessary to refer the matter to the Office for the Supervision of Solicitors. That threat worked. The paperwork arrived shortly afterwards.

I was told that a specialist barrister had been asked to assess the likelihood of winning such a case, and after carrying out his research, he found that a precedent had already been set: it was impossible to sue social services. The barrister said that a similar case had already gone as far as the House of Lords, and they had decreed that social services must never be sued for damage caused during the execution of their normal functions. Social workers, it was claimed, must not feel under threat of being sued, because this could impair their work.

My heart felt like it had been squeezed in a vice. I took this to mean that social services could do whatever they pleased, and you are powerless in law to stop them or take action against them!

Is this why you hear so many horror stories about social workers acting in a way that normal people would consider inhumane? I wondered. This explained a lot. Social services are allowed to do as they please without the possibility of action being taken against them, so this has given them the sense that anything and everything they do is correct. This, in turn, has made them believe they are infallible; that they never make mistakes. Therefore, if something does go wrong – well, it must be down to someone else and not them. God help anyone who challenges them; because if they turn on you, it seems that God is the only one who *could* help you. What a blow.

After the disappointment of hearing that I couldn't take legal action against the social workers, I accepted the fact that they can act with impunity. I had to move on; you cannot allow yourself to become obsessed with unpleasant past events, or you run the risk of becoming bitter and twisted (like a social worker, dare I say).

I tried to put it behind me – to forget the idea. I never even thought about the mountain of paperwork that had been given to the solicitors. It was only after about a year that it came to mind, and I decided that it would be best to try and get this paperwork back. I contacted the London solicitors, who said that it had been sent back to the previous solicitor, because they had retained the bulk of the file. When I contacted the previous solicitor, they said they no longer had any of the paperwork connected to my case, as it had all gone to London and nothing had come back to them.

This was getting ridiculous! I contacted the London solicitor again and they told me that they had only received the minimum of paperwork from the previous solicitor. After it had been decided that I could not pursue a case against social services, everything they held had been returned by document exchange (DX) to the previous solicitor! I am not sure how DX works – but not too well, it would seem, since my documents had either disappeared, or someone had destroyed them.

Still, *I couldn't sue the social workers, so why worry about the paperwork?* I thought, and that was the end of that.

Meanwhile, two years after the local authority said they would investigate Sally's assault by Mrs Bell, in 1 June 1998, an investigation was finally carried out by a Pupil Exclusion and Mediation Officer. As far as they were concerned, they had found nothing wrong. Here are a couple of extracts from this investigation:

The decision not to interview *SALLY* in connection to the alleged complaint was made in consultation with Social Services.

Obviously at some stage, a decision was reached that there would be no interview with *SALLY* in relation to your allegation.

I contacted the local authority and said I was not satisfied with this report and that in my opinion, this investigation was merely an attempt to cover up the assault. I wanted it escalated.

A second investigation took place on 23 March 1999, some ten months later, and this one was carried out by a Consumer Relations Officer. The covering letter stated that the investigation was a "STAGE 3 CORPORATE COMPLAINT INVESTIGATION", and it was signed by the Chief Executive.

This is an extract taken from the interview with the school's headmistress, Mrs Phillips:

In line with procedures Mrs *PHILLIPS* had contacted Social Services and the Assistant Education Officer. *MS ARCHER* had discussed it with her line manager and advised Mrs *PHILLIPS* not to interview *SALLY* as she was a very disturbed child and in a delicate state emotionally due to what was going on at home and difficulties at school. If *SALLY* were to be interviewed, and there were doubts as to whether Social Services would allow it, any meeting would be deferred until after the court hearing in May. Mrs *PHILLIPS* said that her feeling and that of others at the time, was that Mr Jordan was trying to discredit Mrs *BELL* because she was being called as a witness at the court hearing.

This is the alleged abuser, Mrs Bell's response to the investigation interview:

she had great difficulty in getting *SALLY* to talk at all. She hardly spoke to the other children and almost never to Mrs *BELL* even when asked a direct question. Mrs *PHILLIPS* had asked her in March 96 about the incident but she had been unable then to recall it. After all this time it was difficult to remember details, but she recalls discussing it with *MR —* the county council solicitor and with *SALLY'S* Guardian ad Litem and presumed, when she heard no more, that the matter had been dealt with.

The last person to be interviewed in the report was the child protection worker, Kathleen Archer, and this is what she said:

When Mrs *Phillips* rang (MS *Archer*) in March 96 about Mr Jordan's complaint *Archer* discussed it with her line manager *MS Ralph*. They concluded that it was not a child protection issue was of a relatively minor nature and could not be substantiated by medical or other evidence they felt that to interview her about this would in itself constitute an abuse

Archer was asked if she could explain Mrs *Phillips* letter of 19 March 96 to Mr Jordan in which she said that a meeting with *Sally* would be deferred until the middle of May at the earliest, when it was anticipated that care proceedings would have been concluded. *Archer* didn't know why Mrs *Phillips* had written this unless it was that she had misunderstood what *Archer* told her. This was that they could not investigate the complaint because it concerned an issue directly relating to the court case; namely, that Mr Jordan was saying that *Sally's* problems were the result of abuse at school and Social Services were saying they were the result of her home life.

The conclusion:

The meeting with *Sally* did not take place and Mrs *Phillips* who seems to have been waiting for a lead from Social Services, did not follow it up. However, the guidelines are clear. When a complaint is not proceeding any further down a child protection or criminal prosecution route, the Headteacher should initiate a meeting with the teacher concerned and an officer of the LEA to consider the allegations. If, as a result of this meeting, there are no grounds for any disciplinary action, the matter is concluded. It appears that Mrs *Phillips* did not initiate this meeting because, presumably, she was expecting to continue her enquiries with *Sally* once the Care Proceedings had ended. But as these weren't concluded until February 1997 and she retired in March 97 no further action was ever taken.

Although I have upheld Mr Jordan's complaint that there were shortcomings in the process of dealing with his complaint, I do not believe that they affected the outcome; this was determined by delay and Mr Jordan must accept a measure of responsibility for this.

Chapter 15

Some years later, in 2013, I saw a television news report in which a senior social worker was being interviewed about what was going wrong with the service, in the light of the number of high-profile child tragedies reported in recent years. Why was the system failing so many children?

The reply the social worker gave made me feel sick to my stomach.

"Government cuts to funding," was the answer.

Social workers being overworked and underpaid was basically the reason she was giving!

"When a social worker returns to the office after a hard day's work," she said, "they can't always find a desk to sit at immediately. And even if they do, then, they often have to share a computer."

You what?

So, was she saying that children are at risk because a social worker doesn't have their own desk to sit at, and they sometimes have to wait for a computer to become available? Always someone else's fault, never theirs! A social worker will never,

ever admit to making a mistake.

I can understand why social workers think this way. They have been given almost unlimited power, as far as children and families are concerned; they cannot be held to account by law, and judges almost always support their views, no matter how twisted they may seem to the average person in the street. Their dealings all take place in secrecy, and because the children's division of social services has become dominated by workers who support this way of working, newly trained staff either have to become the same... or leave. If they don't comply, they don't last. Another reason social workers believe they don't make mistakes, which I've mentioned before, is that when they've become involved with a family, they believe there definitely is a problem with that family. Their further twisted logic is that if you disagree with them, for whatever reason – to them, this shows that you're in denial, and simply won't accept the problems they reckon you have. Not that they could be wrong, themselves.

When the senior social worker on the news was asked about social worker staffing levels, she said the biggest problem was staff retention. Ask yourself why! Usually, people go into this type of profession because they feel a desire to help people and families who need help. What happens when a caring level-headed person trains for this type of work, and then finds themselves working alongside experienced, embittered social workers? People who, to me, seem to be some of the most damaged individuals you will ever come across? The caring new recruit can either change themselves to become like the longstanding workers, in whom common sense caring seems not to exist – or they can leave. And, as was said in the interview, many of them leave.

As the months rolled on, the psychiatrist decided that Martha was making good progress and therefore instructed the nurse who administered the medication to begin decreasing the dosage – until she would be off the medication completely. This was great news, that we tentatively hoped would end up well. Over time, as the dosage was being decreased, I could see Martha becoming more normal – back to how she had been when I first met her – her younger self. When she was on a strong dosage of medication, she had glazed eyes and would move like a zombie, and she had been on a strong dosage for a long time. To see her gradually regaining her old self – moving like an ordinary person and acting in a normal manner, after so long, was quite a relief!

Over a period of about twelve months, the medication was reduced gradually until it was stopped completely, and the psychiatrist said that Martha was now better and no longer needed his help! He closed his file on her.

It was absolutely fantastic to have a normal family, and to be able to do normal things – and most importantly, to be able to relax at home. Unfortunately, this normality was short-lived.

Within two months of the psychiatrist closing Martha's case, I began to see little signs of her abnormal behaviour returning. Things such as her carrying a bag that contained food and drink with her wherever she went. Martha believed that if the food and drink was out of sight for the shortest period of time, it would allow the neighbours an opportunity to tamper with it.

As time went on, to my dismay, her symptoms became more extreme. She frequently looked wary, her eyes flicking from side to side, hyper-aware of any possible perceived threats. She would mutter small conspiracy theories to me, her paranoia increasing.

"They've fitted cameras inside the television," she would whisper to me, her eyes wide and wild.

"Who?" I asked, the first time. I soon came to know who she meant, as she accused them with grim regularity.

"Them!" She jerked her thumb towards the right-hand party-wall adjoining the neighbours' house and leant forward, confidentially, to hiss at me: "They've put cameras in. So they can watch me."

No amount of reassurance I gave her, evidence otherwise I showed her, or distraction I attempted would dissuade her. She fitted extra locks and bolts on all the doors, and even on some of the cupboard doors, just in case the neighbours had made an entranceway in the back of the cupboard.

On several occasions, our daughter Rachel would say that while she was with Martha in a shop, "Mum said the shop lights were flashing as she walked under them. She said this means there must be cameras fitted in them, that are monitoring her."

A few times, Rachel said, "Mum went over to one or two of the shop assistants and asked why the lights flashed whenever she walked under them."

She would also say to Rachel that people were looking at them or watching them.

"Oh, Dad," Rachel said, rubbing her face with her hand. "It's dead embarrassing to go out with Mum. Can't you do anything?"

Martha had also begun to openly shout and swear at the neighbours, accusing them of fitting cameras in our house so that they could spy on her.

I decided to go to the doctor and tell her that Martha's symptoms were back and that she needed to go back on her medication. She had been fine a few weeks earlier, on her low dosage, but now, her symptoms were creeping back, so she clearly needed something to keep her well.

But when I told the doctor she simply said, "I'm sorry, but I can't just do that. You can't come on her behalf. Martha will have to make an appointment herself to see me. And then, I can refer her back to the psychiatrist."

"But Martha won't come to see you," I said. "She thinks there's nothing wrong with her! She reckons it's other people that have a problem."

The doctor asked me for Martha's date of birth and then brought up Martha's file on the computer.

"Hmm," she said, reading quickly, a blank look on her face, but her forehead wrinkled in concentration. She turned back from the screen. "No. I can still do nothing unless Martha comes herself and asks for help."

"Oh, but I just said..."

"I can tell you that there's a note in Martha's file that says that you are the only reason the children have not been taken into care," she told me. "And there's another to say that social services asked Martha's neighbours to keep an eye on her."

"What?" I said, stunned.

The doctor folded her hands and said, "With all that's gone on within the family, it's a pity you hadn't been able to enjoy the children while they were small."

I frowned. *Was that a threat?* Was I paranoid, now?

I told her I would ask Martha to make an appointment and left the doctors' surgery, still frowning in puzzlement and concern.

The situation seemed totally ridiculous. If I told Martha that she needed to go to the doctors, she would say the same thing as she always said: that there was nothing wrong with her; the problem was with other people.

I came to a halt, mid-footstep. A sudden thought had stopped me in my tracks: what was that the doctor had said?

"Social services had asked Martha's neighbours to keep an eye on her."

This meant that social workers must have gone to our neighbours and discussed with them certain things that should surely be private! They would not just go to Martha's neighbours and ask them to keep an eye on her without giving some reason for it! What had they said, and what had they implied, or left unsaid? What a way to start neighbours gossiping! As most of us know, as gossip spreads, the story gets exaggerated with each new person who is told.

Should social workers have discussed Martha's private details with neighbours who were strangers to her, and then asked these strangers to spy on her? Were social workers even allowed, by law, to discuss someone's private details with strangers – even if they *were* neighbours?

But this is the most worrying thing: Martha had been diagnosed as suffering from severe paranoia, with symptoms that included a conviction that her neighbours were spying on her. But – wait a minute! Her neighbours *had been* spying on her!

Social workers had asked them to! Obviously, the neighbours had not gone to the lengths to spy on her that Martha had believed – fitting cameras in our house or coming in through secret panels in the walls, to poison her food and drink. But it did explain the neighbours calling out at her over the garden fence, "We know all about you!" and threatening that if she stepped out of line, they would report her.

Her paranoia was justifiable!

It would appear that the social workers had been fuelling Martha's illness!

Whether this was just inappropriate practice, stupidity, or something more sinister, I will probably never know; but anyone with an ounce of common sense knows that you don't put out a fire by throwing petrol on it. Nor would you ask strangers to spy on someone who suffers from severe paranoia – especially about neighbours spying on her – unless you wish to exacerbate the illness! My blood ran cold in my veins, as the true situation revealed itself.

It also raised the question of how much of this paranoia was in Martha's head and how much was really going on, in actual fact!

My mind whirled. What would it take? How

many instances of seeing neighbours spying on her and hearing them threatening to report her, before a fragile person cracked, and old fears and paranoia arose again?

Would social services' interference and persecution never stop?

I could speculate endlessly about the rights and wrongs of things, but I had to try and find a solution to the problem that seemed to be getting worse by the day. I decided to call the psychiatric hospital and speak to the psychiatrist.

I was put through to the psychiatrist's secretary who told me, "I'm afraid there's nothing we can do unless Martha is referred to us by her doctor."

I explained what was happening with Martha and that there was no way on earth she would go to the doctor about the problem.

The psychiatrist's secretary said, "Hmmm. I can see you're in an awkward position. Most people with a mental health problem *know* they have a problem. So, they're more willing to comply and seek help."

"But the very nature of Martha's condition is that she thinks the problem lies with other people!"

The psychiatrist's secretary said, "Well, I'm

sorry, but if she won't see a doctor... the only thing you can do is wait..."

"Wait? Wait for what?"

"Until Martha tries to hurt someone, or herself... Then she could be sectioned. Or until the situation with the neighbours gets so bad that the police decide to intervene..."

"You have to be joking!" I was basically being told that Martha could not be helped until she attacked someone! What a state of affairs this was!

She apologised, but said there was nothing else she could advise.

You are on your own, Jack! Come back when you have a knife between your ribs and then, maybe, we can do something. Great.

Chapter 16

Things went from bad to worse. Because of Martha's erratic behaviour, the children wouldn't bring friends to the house through sheer embarrassment. I approached the doctor several times and said that Martha's condition had deteriorated; but, still, no help was forthcoming. I eventually phoned the psychiatric hospital again, and again they said they could do nothing. However, the nurse did suggest trying a different doctor, to see if they would help.

So, I did just that. I called the surgery to make an appointment and asked to see a different doctor.

The new doctor seemed very sympathetic as I explained everything that had happened and what was happening now. But, like the previous doctor, he also told me that without Martha's consent, he could do nothing.

My voice rose, in exasperation. "So, you're saying that I have to wait until she tries something terrible, like killing someone, before she can get help?"

The doctor hesitated for a few moments,

staring at my anxious face, and then said, "However, from what you've told me, I would assume that Martha is in a mental state such that she is no longer capable of making a rational decision for herself. So, based on that, I will make a report that she needs to be assessed by a mental health team."

I breathed out heavily. "Thank you."

Some light at the end of the tunnel! Some hope, at last.

The doctor advised that I would probably receive a call from a mental health worker to arrange for the assessment to take place. What a relief! Something was finally going to be done!

The next day, I got a call from a psychiatric nurse, who said that a team of professionals would come to the house to see Martha to assess whether or not she needed help. The nurse told me that the doctor who had referred Martha would also attend. The appointment was set for the following day at 12.30 p.m.

"Is that definite?" I asked. "I mean, is that a precise time?" I had visions of when you get told a delivery or a repairman will be with you somewhere between the hours of 12 and 6pm. There's no way I could cope with that. As long as I knew the time, I could make sure Martha wasn't out shopping or anything. This needed to go like clockwork, and I could make sure she was there at the house, unsuspecting – until they arrived to do the assessment.

She said they would be punctual and that they would need me there, at the house, to let them in, which I said would be fine.

"I'll have to come home from work, anyway and make sure she's in. But definitely 12.30 on the dot – yeah? I can't really keep her in all afternoon, if they're late. Or even if she gets suspicious..."

"Yes. 12.30. Prompt," she assured me.

So, the next day, at 12 noon, I went home from work – which was most unusual for me.

"Hiya!" I said, to her surprise.

She frowned. "What? What are you doing home?"

"Ach, I thought I'd pop over, seeing's it's lunchtime," I told Martha. "I've left a document I need - on the computer, here. I might as well to do some work on it, up in the bedroom."

"Oh," she said, dully, her brow still furrowed.

Upstairs, I pulled a chair close to the bedroom window and watched the minutes pass, nervously glancing out now and again. And when the time came to just before 12.30 p.m., I saw a car pull up just down the road. I took a quick intake of breath. *This must be them!* At exactly 12.30 p.m., someone got out of the car and looked around them. It was the doctor. It seemed as if he was looking to see if the other professionals had arrived, but because there were no other cars close by, he got back into his car. I was wondering where on earth they all were, too, my heart beating hard in my chest.

At about 12.40 p.m., ten minutes after the team was supposed to be there, I saw the doctor get out of his car again, and he walked over to our house. I scrambled up from my chair and thundered downstairs, to get to the door before Martha did, just as he knocked on our door.

I cautiously opened the front door and pulled a face, shrugging my shoulders to indicate that I had no idea what was going on – or why the team weren't there, promptly, as I'd been assured.

The doctor muttered quietly to me, "Aren't they here, yet?"

"No," I replied, feeling sweat trickle down my neck. "They promised they'd be here on time, too."

Then, having heard us talking, Martha came to the door, loomed over my shoulder and spotted the doctor. "Who are you?" she demanded, her face dark with suspicion.

And, of course, the doctor had to tell her who he was.

"A doctor?" Martha asked, her eyes narrowing in anger and concern. "What are you doing here?"

"I wanted to talk to you."

"There's nothing wrong with me! So, you're wasting your time!" she snapped, and rushed down the hallway.

"Well, let's just have a chat, then," said the doctor, stepping in after her.

But Martha grabbed her coat off the hook, went out of the back door and carried on, scurrying down the garden, and out through the back gate.

"Should I go after her?" I asked. "Only, I can't very well rugby tackle her and drag her back."

"Let's wait. We'd need to wait for the team, anyway."

The doctor and I stood talking for a while, wondering what had happened to the psychiatric team, who had said they would be at the house at 12.30 p.m., prompt. I was growing increasingly concerned and agitated. It was now nearly 12.50 p.m.

Then, at that point, three cars arrived together and parked about 50 yards up the road. The doctor and I were now standing in the street, having gone to look out for them. As the people got out of their cars and came walking down the road holding papers and clipboards, they were casually talking amongst themselves, and laughing together, quite blithely, as if nothing was wrong at all.

Approaching us, one of them asked, "Where is she, then?"

"She left the house when I arrived, at 12.40 p.m," the doctor said.

"We expected you twenty minutes ago," I snapped. "… when she was still here."

"Yeah, well, we went down the wrong road," one of the team said, apparently nonplussed. "And then, we couldn't find the house."

Two of them looked at each another, one shrugging. Another shook his head and sighed heavily. "Well! If she's not here, then, there's nothing we can do."

"She won't be far away!" I told them, grabbing my coat, ready to jump in a car. "She'll have headed towards town. If we drive up the road, we'll probably see her!"

"No, we can't do that," replied one of the

team. "If she's not on the property, we can't do the assessment."

"But... you..." I was speechless.

And that was that. They got back into their cars. And off they went.

The doctor shook his head in amazement at what had just happened. "I'm sorry," he said awkwardly, his lips twisted in an apologetic grimace. "But there's nothing else I can do now."

It was absolutely unbelievable! Were they completely incompetent? Or was it that they just didn't give a damn about a person with a mental health problem? Why would they handle things in such a casual manner?

We were back in the same nightmarish situation, in which Martha thought everyone was watching her. She believed that the police, doctors, social workers, neighbours were trying to make out she was mad. And now, even I was. I couldn't blame her, really. I understood why she would think that social workers were trying to prove she was mad, because of their behaviour during our previous involvement with them. I could also see why she would suspect the neighbours, too – because in the past, the neighbours appeared to know more about

Martha than they should have known. They had even told her, "We know all about you!" Again, I think this was down to the actions of the social workers. That, and them asking the neighbours to literally keep an eye on her for them...

We had moved properties many times over the years, due to Martha's behaviour, but we had been in this last house for some years by then, and I was not about to move again. As you can imagine, neighbours came and went. By this time, it was around 2003 or 2004, and a young couple moved in next door. I got on with them very well, and since they weren't at home a lot of the time, Martha was not quite as bad with them. Mind you, after about twelve to eighteen months, they told me they had put in for a house exchange. They said it wasn't because of Martha, but with them mentioning her at all, I imagine it probably was.

They moved out and a woman moved in. Since she tended to stay at home a lot, it was not long before the fun and games began. A lot of shouting would go on between Martha and the neighbour, but because I was at work during the day I didn't know the full extent of it. However, I know that the police were called out many times, sometimes by Martha and at other times, by the neighbour.

I happened to bump into the neighbour in the local shop, and she asked me, "What's the matter with your missus? Why's she taken against me, so bad? It's like she hates me – and I've done nothing!"

"It's not you," I said, and I told her that Martha was like that with all the neighbours, unfortunately.

"Great," she said with a sigh, as I held the door open for her, before following her out of the shop.

We fell into step together and while we were walking back home, the neighbour made me laugh. "Them I swapped with, who used to live next to you... They told me they had good neighbours on both sides!" she cried. "But... good for what?"

It seemed that the young couple she'd made the house exchange with might not have been entirely truthful about their neighbours. When our new neighbour moved in, she found that she had Martha on one side, shouting at her whenever she saw her in the day, and a woman on the other side, who played loud music all night.

"No rest for the wicked, they say! What did I do to deserve this? I must be very, very, bad indeed!"

It was how she said it, that just seemed so funny!

So, it seemed that the young couple had probably moved because the woman on the other side of them was playing loud music at night. I thought, *Good thing Martha can't hear it...* Or there'd have been another neighbour calling the police!

Although that was a light-hearted exchange in part, things didn't improve.

Chapter 17

Time moved on and the situation between Martha and the neighbour was getting worse. I was also feeling worn down by walking on egg-shells every day and having lived with someone over many years who was erratic and irrational for much of the time, I had to think about the children and myself. It was hard, but the woman I'd loved and supported over the years; the mother of my children, was no longer recognisable – and it was an impossible life for us all. I'd tried everything. I'd got no help from any quarter, and the situation was dire. Rachel and John were now aged fourteen and fifteen, growing up fast, but Martha was causing trouble in the neighbourhood and embarrassing them so that they never wanted to be at home, let alone bring friends round. We'd responded in the past by moving, but that didn't solve anything. The problems just recurred in a different setting. And I was tired. So tired. I'd thought about this for a long time... on many occasions. So, I decided that it was time to make a break from their mother.

"Dad, you can't just leave us with her," Rachel said. "It's not fair."

Both children said that they wanted to remain with me rather than stay with Martha because of how she was acting towards everyone. And besides, we'd been there for years and were settled – it was too much upheaval for the kids.

So, I sat Martha down, and explained how I felt, and what the children wanted, and we discussed the situation, as best we could. She was sad and disappointed, but hardly surprised, since we had grown apart over the years. She also appreciated that her mental health issues and past record meant that she wasn't really in a position to look after the children, alone. Since we lived in a council house and the tenancy was solely in my name, I told Martha that I wanted her to move out. It seemed the best way – to give the children stability and security.

She nodded sadly, but agreed, "I know. It's probably for the best."

Besides, the neighbours were still spying on her. She wanted to move.

"It's okay, the council will sort you out a place," I said. And I gave Martha a letter to take to the council stating that I wanted her to move out, which she took and showed to the housing department.

243

On her return, she told me that when she showed them the letter, "They said it would be best if I applied to the court myself, to take the tenancy away from you."

"What?"

"They reckon because I've got two children, the court would almost certainly transfer the tenancy to me – because they won't make a mother with two kids homeless."

And they also told her that, due to the fact that I would then be classed as a single male, and the council would have no obligation to house me.

"But I told them…" Martha explained, "about all the run-ins we've had with social services in the past, and my mental health history. I said if it got to court, it's more than likely it'd be you that's awarded custody of the children."

I nodded. This was what we'd discussed.

She went on: "The council worker said, in that case, they could offer no help with accommodation and I would have to stay where I am."

I shook my head, in despair. "But that's not going to work."

She said, sheepishly, "They told me that if you went to court and got me evicted… then I could go back to the council and they would reconsider the situation. Maybe have to find me somewhere."

After she told me that, I sat, grim-faced, thinking of the possibilities. Of which, there was only one option. The next day, I contacted a solicitor to explore the possibility of getting Martha out of the house. It might seem harsh, but after so many years of being with someone with disturbed behaviour, I just wanted some normality for me and the children.

I explained everything to the solicitor and he said, "Yes, you have grounds to get her out of the house..." Then he paused, holding up one finger, warningly, and looked me in the eye. "But because you're a man trying to remove a woman from the family home, you could be in for a long, drawn-out ride."

My heart sank. He explained, "Normally, it's the woman who applies to remove the man – and it's usually over and done with within a month. But I must warn you – don't expect it to go so easily, for you. The courts don't like to remove women from their children or from the family home."

"Oh, no..." I murmured. "You mean I don't stand much chance?"

"I just mean that everything will have to be

watertight before we go to court."

I nodded. Despite the insecurity, I just felt a sense of relief because the process of removing Martha from the house had begun. I had no choice.

Now, since it was only my name that was on the tenancy agreement, you might think I could have just waited until Martha had left the house to go shopping or something, and then just change the locks. I had thought of doing this, but I'd decided I would wait and see what the solicitor's advice was. It was a good thing I did, too, because the solicitor advised me that if I had simply changed the locks, Martha could have gone to the housing department – who could then have called the police to say that I had unlawfully prevented her from entering her family home – where she and her children were living.

"Although Martha's name is not on the tenancy agreement," the solicitor advised, "because she has lived there for several years, the house is classed as her family home."

Without all the facts about Martha's behaviour and her mental problems, and with only the knowledge that a man was unlawfully preventing a woman from entering her family home, I was likely to be in court within days and it would probably be decided that I was the villain and Martha was the victim. The tenancy would be given to Martha and I would be out on the street. He told me that I must just allow the court to deal with it.

I went home and told Martha, "I've been to see a solicitor and he's begun the process of getting an eviction order against you."

"Eviction?" Her face fell.

"Remember, we talked about it? It seems the only way to make sure they give you housing..."

Although she knew that I intended to take this action, the reality of it and the fact that it had actually begun seemed to aggravate the situation. Of course, it was the neighbour that she took her anger out on.

Shortly after this – I am not sure of the exact date – I got up in the morning, as usual, at about 7.30 a.m. and was just about to wake Martha and the children, when there was a knock on the door.

I ran downstairs and opened it, and there were two men standing there, who introduced themselves as police officers. They were both in plain clothes: white short-sleeved shirts and black trousers. I seem to recall that they were senior CID officers.

"We need to talk to Martha Jordan, please,"

one of them said.

"That's my partner," I frowned, suspiciously. "What about?"

"About complaints we've received from your neighbour," they said.

"And you've come at this hour of the morning?"

"We've called at the house several times, but no one has answered the door. So, we decided to try to catch her in. Is she here?"

"She's upstairs," I told them but I doubted if she would talk to them. They said that they would keep coming back until they did get to talk to her.

"Just a moment, then," I stepped outside and closed the door so Martha wouldn't be able to hear me talking to them. "Listen, we're not actually together," I told them. "In fact, I'm taking legal action to get her out of the house."

It was their turn to eye me suspiciously, but I hoped they could see I was sincere. I said, "If you really want to talk to her, you should drive round to the back of the house and wait. That's where my car's parked. We drive the children to school, so if you wait at the rear of the house, you'll catch her while she's in the car."

We talked in general about Martha's

behaviour towards our Asian neighbours, including the woman currently living next door, which, unfortunately, had included some derogatory comments the neighbour had reported as racism.

"Oh, that's terrible. I can't believe anyone would call us racist!" I cried.

The police officer said, "I can tell you're not a racist, but..."

"I don't believe Martha is racist, either," I explained. "She has mental health issues. She's paranoid. Maybe even still schizophrenic. I'm sure any perceived racist remarks she might have made towards the neighbour would have been misinterpreted. More about her striking back at people she thought were spying on her. Not because of any true racist feelings. Next door are fairly new – they don't know her."

This neighbour would have heard nothing about our family's past from social services, because by this time, the children were no longer on the at-risk register and all our involvement with social services had ceased. But of course, for Martha, every neighbour and almost every other person was spying on her, for the sole purpose of trying to drive her mad. I could hardly blame her – in a way, she was justified in having such feelings, after what had happened to us over the years.

The police officers left to go around to the rear of the house to wait.

After the children and Martha were ready, we got into the car and I drove out of the back gate and stopped in the street. The two police officers got out of their car and came over to us.

"Martha Jordan?" one of them said. "We need to talk to you about your neighbour's complaints and what you've been saying."

I remember the exact words Martha used, because there were not many of them as she replied, "I said nothing, and I am saying nothing."

The police officers asked why she wouldn't give them her side of the story and Martha's reply was: "Because the police tell lies," and those were the only words they could get out of her.

One of the officers then said, "If we can't get your side of the story, all we have to go on is your neighbour's side of things . If you refuse to co-operate, we'll have to file our report based on that."

Martha kept her mouth firmly closed, and was informed that she would receive a court summons through the post in due course.

Chapter 18

It took a few weeks for the court summons to arrive. Martha said she was not interested in opening it, so I did.

I read it, and my blood ran cold. I had to read it again, in disbelief. I was shocked by what it contained. It stated that when asked by the police officer at the rear of the property why she was abusive to the neighbour, Martha had replied, "I called them fucking Paki bastards because they are fucking Paki bastards."

It stated that these comments had been witnessed by the other police officer and that, as a result, Martha was being charged with aggravated racism!

I could not believe it! The police had falsified the statement! Now, whether or not Martha had made these comments to the neighbours at some other time, I don't know, but the police statement said that she made these comments right in front of them – and she most definitely had not! Ironically, one of the few things Martha *had* said to the police officers was "The police tell lies," and they had clearly just proved her right!

Martha's court date was set for several months later. In the meantime, I had received a court date to apply for her to be removed from the house, set for **10th May, 2007**.

Martha had already been to see various solicitors, seeking their representation at her future court date for the aggravated racism charge. She even travelled to Birmingham to find a solicitor, because she felt that everyone in Bankham was against her and all the professional bodies there were trying to drive her mad.

She told the solicitor about the police statement, and that it was all lies.

The solicitor asked her, "If what you are saying about this falsification is true, then why is your partner, David, not making a statement to support your story? He's a witness."

"Because he's supporting all the people who are trying to drive me mad," Martha said.

In truth, I could not bring myself to make a statement supporting her, because I wanted her out of the house. Unfortunately, for the children's sake, I was prepared to go along with anything that would help me to achieve this goal. My court appointment to obtain the eviction notice was before Martha's court date. I thought that if my application failed, if Martha was convicted of aggravated racism, then surely the local housing authority would go to court themselves to get her out of the house. That was my back-up plan.

On **10 May 2007,** I went to Woodshire Crown Court, with my solicitor. I still had clear memories of this particular court, from the time that Judge Robert Martin had granted the care order on Sally, so for that traumatic reason, I had the idea in my head that I would be subjected to some sort of scathing attack from this judge, too. I felt sick to my stomach at the thought that I might lose my children and my home.

My solicitor and I were led into a side room with a large table and chairs placed in the centre, and a middle-aged judge entered from another door and told us to take a seat. I sat and stared at him, trying to make out which way it might go, with him. He had an open, kindly face, which surprised me. Still, I wasn't about to let my guard down. District Judge Robinson told us that he had read all the details of my application for the removal of Martha from the property and that he wanted to deal with it in an informal manner if possible. I swallowed, feeling myself relax a little.

Judge Robinson said, "I want you to tell me

in your own words all the details why you want the court to issue an eviction notice."

I told him everything I could, my throat dry. I noticed that I was trembling, when he encouraged me to take a glass of water, and I almost spilt it, with my hand shaking.

He also asked me if the children were aware of what I intended to do and if they had expressed a view as to which parent they would like to stay with in the event of their mother leaving the premises.

"Yes," I assured him. "Both children said they want to stay with me." I went on to recount how Martha had behaved over the years, inside and outside the house, and explained that her behaviour was, in my view, a result of mental illness. "It's just not good for the children, either."

We talked for some time, and the judge said, at last, "Well, from what you have told me about her history and behaviour, I am satisfied that Martha is indeed suffering from a mental illness. However, of course, I am no psychiatrist."

He said that mental health law could be a little complex and that although he was satisfied that she was suffering from a mental illness, he did not have the power to order a mental health assessment on her.

"That said, I cannot imagine how it must have been for you and the children over the years, having to live in such an environment." He said, "I feel that you deserve to have a normal home life. Not just in the future, but now."

Judge Robinson said he would issue a twenty-four-hour eviction notice against Martha and, also, an injunction to prevent her returning or coming within 100 metres of the house.

"Do you believe that Martha will comply with the eviction order?" the judge asked me, and I said no. "I concur," he said. "Given her mental illness, I suspect that she would probably ignore the order and hope it went away, or not have the capacity to appreciate its meaning." Judge Robinson said. "We need a safeguard. I suggest that if the eviction order were served by the police, it would have more authority – but if Martha ignored it, then, she would be arrested and could find herself in prison."

I gave a shudder. It seemed extreme, but I couldn't reason with her. Perhaps it was the only way.

"No. We don't want that," he said, rubbing his chin, considering. "There are too many people suffering from mental illness in prisons, when they should be in a hospital, not prison. I will have the eviction order served by an officer of the court. If she leaves on receipt of the order, all well and good. If, however, she does not leave the property, and she probably will not, she will be in contempt of court. This gives the court more powers to deal with her, such as order a mental health report to be completed on her."

My eyes widened. That was clever.

The judge said he wanted to keep her out of the criminal system if he possibly could. He said he would have the eviction notice made straight away, and an injunction to come into force as soon as she left the property. The eviction was to be dealt with by the officer of the court, and the injunction would come under police jurisdiction.

He said he would have to make many notes on the case, because, "If you need to come back to court because she has ignored the eviction order – as she probably will – then it is highly likely that you will see a different judge. If another judge sees that I have issued a twenty-four-hour eviction order on a woman to remove her from the family home, yet the order is not to be enforced by the police, the other judge will think that I myself have mental issues – because such action is never taken. I must therefore make notes to explain why."

The judge wished me luck and left the room. I could hardly prevent myself from smiling, although I was still wary of how this would go, in reality.

My solicitor and I took the paperwork to an office within the court building and had to wait about thirty to forty minutes for the official eviction notice and injunction order to be made. The fact that everything had gone exactly how I'd hoped felt a little unreal, and even though the order had yet to be served on Martha, I was feeling a sense of relief.

We went to collect a copy of the order and the solicitor said it would be best if we waited until Monday for him to serve the order on Martha.

"If the order is served on a Friday, it would make it difficult for the local housing department to deal with it over the weekend," he explained. That was fair enough – we didn't want Martha to be homeless, after all. If he handed it to her at close of play on the Monday, that would give her, and the council, all of Tuesday to be rehoused before her twenty-four hours were up. That was if she complied. If not, the enforcement process would begin.

I had a difficult weekend, half-excited, half

afraid – but in a way, it was the kind of life I was used to, living with Martha.

On Monday, **14 May, 2007,** at approximately 5.30 p.m., the solicitor came to the house and handed the notice of eviction to Martha.

She took it blankly, but she shut down, and said and did nothing. I now had to wait twenty-four hours – and if Martha was still at the property after that, I was to inform the solicitor and he would instruct the court to send an officer to the house to enforce the order.

As expected, Martha ignored the order, so I contacted the solicitor, who, in turn, contacted the court. I now had to wait for an officer of the court to enforce the order.

A week went by and each time I came home from work, Martha was still at the house; so I contacted the solicitor to tell him. The solicitor contacted the court again to ask why the officer of the court had not yet enforced the order. He was told that on every occasion that the officer had attended the house, Martha would not open the door!

"That's ridiculous!" I cried. "What's the idea of enforcing an eviction notice if the person just stays?"

The only option now was to re-apply to the court, which is what Judge Robinson had said would probably have to happen. Life carried on the way it had been – the children steering clear, staying out, seeing friends, and Martha sitting still, occasionally shouting at neighbours, ever paranoid and difficult.

My solicitor applied for another court hearing on the grounds that Martha had disobeyed the order and was thus in contempt of court. Another hearing was set for 10.30 a.m. on **4 July 2007** and Martha was served notice of this. The summons stated that if the court found the contempt of court allegation to be true, Martha would need to "show good reason why she should not be sent to prison". I had no fear of this happening – because the details of my court application documented Martha's mental problems, I was hopeful that the court would order a mental health assessment on her, and she would get help – and another home – at last.

Martha was aware of the court's involvement and I think she realised that it was only a matter of time before she would be physically removed from the house, so her behaviour got worse. The date of her court appearance came, and she did not attend.

I am unsure what the result of her not

attending court was supposed to be, but I believe that officers of the court were instructed to remove her from the property as soon as they were able. It had become difficult because they were still trying to keep the case out of police hands, so as not to criminalise her.

However, the officers of the court never did remove her, because events then took a strange turn.

Chapter 19

On **Thursday, 12 July**, a week after Martha should have attended court, I got up in the morning and woke the children so that they could get ready for school, as usual.

Martha got up and immediately began talking, or rather shouting, about the neighbours. "That bitch! That stinking bitch! She's been at it again! She's been in the house, and she's told the police lies about me!"

She was saying very aggressive things and blaming all the problems that we had on our neighbour. She was enraged. I tried to soothe her and reassure her that things were fine. Everything she was saying, and the way she was saying it, made me very concerned. But I had to go to work and hoped that she would simmer down by herself. She generally did. But still, I had an uncomfortable feeling I couldn't shake off.

I left for work and the children left for school – they were walking to school themselves, by now. Martha stayed in the house, since she very rarely left the house by that point, probably for fear that the officers of the court would grab her. This particular day, she had seemed much more aggressive than usual and it really made me fear that she might do something to the neighbour. I was not sure, of course, but I couldn't take that risk; so, as soon as I got to work, I phoned the police. They had details about us and the problems between Martha and the neighbour all on file, and I explained to them that Martha had seemed very aggressive when I left home.

I warned them that if they received a call from our neighbour concerning Martha that they should take it very seriously and attend as soon as possible. What else could I do?

At about 3.30 p.m., I received a call from my daughter, Rachel. She told me that she and John had just got home, but their mum wasn't there.

I said, "It's OK. She's probably just gone to the shops."

"But her things are still here, in the house!" Rachel said, her voice rising in concern. "Stuff she wouldn't ever leave the house without! Her bag and coat. She never leaves the house without them, Dad!"

So, I knew something was not right.

I work close to home – about 5 minutes' walk or 2 minutes' drive, so I went straight home. It was very strange, going into the house: there was an eerie silence, an atmosphere we had never experienced in the house before, and the children and I found ourselves whispering.

I wondered if something had happened and the police had arrested her, or somehow the enforcement officers had managed to eject her, after all. I must admit, it also felt a little exciting.

I called the solicitor straight away and told him what had happened that morning and how I had informed the police.

"If the police have arrested Martha," I asked, "does that constitute her officially leaving the premises? Because the Court Order stated that as soon as Martha left the premises, the injunction would come into force to prevent her re-entering the property. And it's a criminal offence to break an injunction."

I was unsure of the situation, because the eviction order was intended to be carried out by officers of the court. How would things stand if it had been the police who had eventually removed her?

The solicitor said that it did not matter who removed her – the injunction would still come into force. "But," he said, "make sure she *has* been removed by either the police or the court officers. And then, change the door locks as quick as you possibly can."

The children came with me, back to my workplace, and remained with me while I phoned the police station from the office to try to find out what had happened to Martha. I asked if she had been arrested and was told that due to data protection law they were not able to give me any information whatsoever.

We stayed at my workplace until about 5.30 p.m. and then went home for something to eat, even though none of us were hungry, because a dark cloud of worry hung over us all.

"Where could she be, Dad?" Rachel asked anxiously, her brow wrinkled.

I needed to know if she'd been arrested – so I could change the locks. If she hadn't been, then there was even more reason to be concerned. At about 7.30 p.m., I told the children that we would go to Bankham police station to see if we could get any information, so off we went. I got exactly the same reply: "Sorry, can't help you. Data Protection Act."

So, we went back home, none the wiser. The children were concerned, and we were all bewildered. We just needed to know where she was.

I left it until about 9.30 p.m. Then, I thought, *This is ridiculous, I can't leave it like this.* I phoned the police again and told them the same thing I had earlier, and once more received the same reply.

"OK. I want to report a missing person."

"Who?" the woman on the phone said.

I said, "Martha."

"What if she isn't missing?" the woman on the phone asked.

I told her, "Martha is always at home at this time of night, and it's out of character for her not to be here. She could be floating face down in the lake for all we know," I said. "I'll come to the police station to report her missing."

"Wait a moment," the woman replied. "I'll put the sergeant on."

A few seconds went by, and a male officer came to the phone, saying, "I understand you're concerned about the whereabouts of Martha."

He told me that due to data protection laws he could not give information out, but he said, gently, "I can, however, reassure you that she is safe."

"That's all I wanted to know," I replied. "So,

she's been arrested, and now I can change the locks."

The sympathetic voice suddenly changed to a stern tone. "What do you mean, change the locks?"

"Now I know she's been arrested, I can change the locks so she can't get back in the house."

"You change the locks and you will be in serious trouble!" he warned me.

I was a little shocked by this and asked, "Why?"

"We did remove her from the property but when we release her we'll be bringing her back. And if she can't get in, you'll be in trouble!"

I don't know if it was the panic I felt at hearing this that mobilised me, but I stated sternly, "You bring her back here, and it's *you* that'll be in trouble."

"What do you mean, *I* will be in trouble?" he blustered.

I told him that a twenty-four-hour eviction notice had been served on her on 14 May, and upon her leaving the property, an injunction was to come into force, so she could not come within 100 metres of the property.

"If you bring her back," I warned him, "you

will be assisting her to break the injunction and the law."

"You can't possibly have an eviction notice and an injunction," he said. "Or we would know about it – because we have to carry them out! And how could you possibly get a twenty-four-hour eviction notice? A court would not give one against a woman – especially not without us knowing about it!"

"Well, I have."

"Do you have copies of the paperwork with you?"

"Yes, I do," I replied.

"I'll send an officer round straight away, to check," he said.

Less than ten minutes later, the police were at the door. I showed the officer the paperwork and he got on his radio. I heard him say, "Yes, the paperwork seems to be in order."

The officer then asked me, "Can I take these papers with me? They need them at the station."

"No... I don't think so..." I felt reluctant to let them out of my hands. "I would prefer to keep them with me."

"I need to make copies of them for my colleagues at the police station," he told me. "I promise I'll have them back to you within the hour."

I agreed. After all, my solicitor and the court had copies.

He was true to his word and was back within the hour. He told me that his colleagues in the police station couldn't understand how I had managed to get a twenty-four-hour eviction notice issued against a woman without them being aware of it. I explained about Martha's behaviour and mental illness, and that a judge had dealt with it this way to try to keep Martha out of the criminal justice system.

When I mentioned Martha's mental state, the police officer said, "Ah! Yes – we thought there was something not quite right with how she was acting."

The officer then went outside and began talking on his radio. After a few minutes, he came back into the house and said, "I've explained what you told me to the officers at the police station. The police doctor is already with Martha. On hearing what you've said, the doctor is arranging for a psychiatric team to come to the station to assess her."

At last! She would be getting the help she needed. It was a pity it had to come to that, but we could rest easy, now. I thought.

After the officers left, I put the children to bed and watched television to try to relax. At about 11.45 p.m., the phone rang. It was a mental health social worker, who told me that a psychiatric team had assessed Martha and decided that she should be sectioned under the Mental Health Act.

I gave an audible sigh of relief, all the tension in my shoulders loosening and dropping.

The mental health worker said that they were arranging transport to take Martha to a psychiatric hospital in Pennyminster and asked whether I wanted to go with her.

"I'm sorry, I can't, because the children are in bed. I've got no-one to look after them, and I can't bring them with me, now. They've got school in the morning. I'm trying to keep things as normal as possible for them."

That was a joke, because nothing about our family life over the years had even vaguely resembled 'normal'.

I told the mental health worker that I would phone Pennyminster Hospital and arrange to take the children to see their mother at a more convenient time.

But, as it happened, the next day, Martha phoned me to say that she was being transferred to

Ravencroft Hospital, a small psychiatric unit on the same site as the main Bankham Hospital. She said she would phone me when she had been moved and would let me know when I could bring the children to visit her.

The children's lives, and my life, reached some semblance of normality.

Martha spent about two months in the hospital, and she was put on medication, there. When the time came for the doctors to say she could leave, there was the problem of where she should go. I told the hospital that there was an injunction to stop her returning to the house – and I said that even if there hadn't been an injunction, the children and I had decided that it would be better if she lived somewhere else.

"We had enough trouble getting her to this point," I explained. "We had real problems getting her removed from the house, so I daren't allow her back to live with us in case her symptoms come back." I also said that the court would not take too kindly to me going back to them a second time, saying that I allowed her back in, and then wanted her out again.

Martha had been allocated a social worker who said she would contact the housing department. And soon, Martha was given a flat to live in.

Life at home became more normal for me and the children. We could relax, and they felt comfortable enough to bring friends back to the house again. Martha seemed relatively normal for quite some time too, and her medication was reduced and eventually stopped.

But once again, not long after her course of medication ended, the children and I could see that her symptoms were returning. I phoned the Psychiatric Unit to tell them what was happening, and they said that because Martha's treatment had finished, there was nothing they could do without it going through Martha's doctor first.

It turned out that she had changed doctors and her old doctor said that I would need to contact her current doctor. I didn't know who that was, and Martha's old doctor couldn't tell me, either. Once again, we were stuck with nowhere to go for help.

It was obvious that the children were concerned about their mother, but I was powerless, exhausted from years of worry, and I told them that we were just going round in circles, trying to get help for her.

"We're just banging our heads against a brick

wall," I said. "She's recently been sectioned under the Mental Health Act, so the hospital are aware of her, the doctor is aware of it, the police and the housing authority are aware. And your mum has a social worker. She is surrounded by specialists, and it's their responsibility, not ours, any more. So, let's let them deal with it. If Martha makes her new neighbours lives hell – and she will – let *them* phone the police. Let *them* phone the council. Let other people take some responsibility, for a change. Because I am sick to death of trying to get help for her when all the response I get is, 'we cannot do anything, we cannot do anything'!"

In recent years, there have been tragic stories in the news about certain mentally ill people attacking someone in the street and, tragically, even killing innocent people. The questions that always follow are: how did it happen? Why was this person allowed to walk the streets? If this person was mentally ill, why were they not in hospital? Well, now you know why they were not in hospital.

It seems to me that, even today, the mere mention of mental illness ensures that a situation is always someone else's job to deal with, but no one deals with it until the police become involved. By this time, the situation is far worse than it ever should have been allowed to become. Just as the judge told me, there are far too many people in prison who shouldn't be there, because of their mental health problems. So, what happens to them? Because they don't receive treatment for their illness, there, they serve their time and when released, they repeat the same conduct that put them in prison in the first place. It's a vicious circle.

Only after the police became involved again was Martha put back on medication. But when you think of the misery this caused people – family, neighbours, everyone involved – just to get a person back on an even keel, you have to ask – why?

My children are adults now. They see their mother several times a week and they often meet up in the town and go shopping together or go to a café. Martha occasionally comes to our house for a Sunday meal. So, yes, life is relatively normal now.

Our eldest daughter, Sally, says she remembers leaving Oldenhurst First School and going to Hillsway Middle School. After she was placed with foster parents, she was taken to school and collected from it by taxi, and some of the older children began to pick on her. For this reason, she wasn't too upset when she was told that social services were moving her to a different school, although she didn't like the idea of leaving her schoolfriends. Some years after leaving school, Sally was talking to one of her old Hillsway school friends on Facebook, who told her that the older children had begun to pick on her purely because they had found out that Sally had been put into care.

Sally now works in a secure mental health facility for young people, of all places. She has spoken to senior members of staff about her past and said their response was pure disbelief at how her mother had been treated by social services, all those years ago. Sally's colleagues were not surprised that her mother had developed mental health issues.

Even if someone like Martha suffers any ill effect due to social workers carrying out their work, the person cannot take legal action against social services because of the House of Lords ruling. However, it seems that the children whom social services are supposed to protect *can* take legal action, if social services' actions can be shown to have caused the child injury in any way; whether physical or emotional harm.

Chapter 20

I saw a case on television, where a young woman was taking legal action on the basis that her family was known to social services when she was a young child, but social services had allowed her to remain with her family. She now considered this decision to have not been in her best interests. She felt that she should have been removed for her own safety.

This made me think about Sally's removal in **Jan 1997,** on the grounds of emotional abuse. Social services' case was based on a statement made by one of Sally's previous teachers, Mrs Bell, describing Sally as a very quiet, shy and isolated little girl who was unable to relate to other children, and reported that, if spoken to, Sally would assume a near-foetal position. Sally's version of events in the classroom were that she had lots of friends and was always talking. However, on one occasion, after she had been told by Mrs Bell to stop talking and had not done so, Mrs Bell made Sally come to the front of the class, where she shook her so hard that her arms hurt for the rest of the day, and she was frightened of the teacher from then, on.

As I've mentioned, I had made a complaint to the school and to Kathleen Archer, the child protection worker; but the school wrote to me to say that they had been instructed by Archer that Sally was not even to be interviewed about it. This was clearly a case of physical assault, and yet the reply from Archer was, whatever the teacher may have done to Sally it was insignificant, compared to the abuse she has suffered at home! Archer completely refused to see what I was trying to get at. If a teacher described a child as so badly damaged that she couldn't communicate with other children – how could she need to be shaken hard for non-stop talking in front of the class? I made an allegation of assault at the time. I have the papers from the school and local authority stating that Sally was never to be interviewed about it. In one paper, Kathleen Archer actually says that if Sally is interviewed about the incident she considered this to constitute child abuse! Looking back now, I would have thought the alleged assault was a criminal offence, and every alleged case of assault, especially on a child, should be investigated. For social services to say that Sally should not to be spoken to about it and that anyone who did talk to her about it would face being accused of child abuse! That, in my opinion, was a clear and deliberate attempt to cover up the assault so that social services could use the teacher's statement. I could never forgive or forget them for breaking up my family, and effectively causing Martha a lifetime of trauma and mental illness, to the detriment of my children, myself, and even the local community, given Martha's erratic behaviour with neighbours. After all these years, I still seethed at the injustice of it all.

Sally still remembers the shaking incident and I still have the paperwork saying she was not to be interviewed about it. It was so unfair and unjust – and it had ruined lives, especially Sally's! So, in early **2013,** I decided to seek legal advice to see if Sally could take action against social services for refusing to investigate the allegation against her teacher, which had effectively led to Sally going into care.

The solicitor said because the police had not been informed at the time of the incident, I would need to contact them now and see how they responded. He said that if the police took up the case, he would also consider taking it on, but I must see how the police responded first.

I phoned the police and gave them the

details of what had happened and when it had happened, and they asked why I had not contacted them at the time.

I replied, "Social services were involved, and I reported the incident to them and the school. I thought that was the route to take."

With all that was going on at the time, I just didn't think to report it to the police.

The police said that because social services were involved at the time of the incident, there was nothing the police could do. I was told that if I was not satisfied with what happened at the time, I should have gone through the social services complaints procedure. I told them I had done that, but social services would not pursue the allegation. The police simply told me to try again.

Thinking about it later, if Kathleen Archer from child protection services said that interviewing Sally about the incident would be considered child abuse, if I *had* reported it to the police, how could they have talked to Sally without committing child abuse, according to social services? What a twisted world this child protection system seemed to have created!

During the process of writing this book, I thought it would be useful to get as much paperwork as possible from social services. You have the legal right to see any information that the authority hold on you, and they are required by law to make copies available to you within a certain time frame. A large part of my paperwork had been lost between solicitors, so I asked my eldest daughter to write to the local authority to ask for copies of all the paperwork they had on her, and especially a copy of the doctor's report and x-ray report that had led to her removal, as a baby.

Some years ago, I had applied in writing, myself, to the local authority to get copies of any paperwork that they held, but they gave me excuse after excuse as reasons why I could not see copies of their files: people were on holiday, people were off ill, experts would have to decide what I could and could not see, and then, there was the large amount of paperwork involved. I think, by law, they have to comply with your request within about forty days, but, of course, this was social services I was dealing with and we know how the law applies to them...

After about a year of writing complaints to them and receiving every excuse they could give, they finally came up with a definitive reason why I could not see any documents. And their reason was good. So good, in fact, that it stopped me dead in my tracks. I was informed that I was only allowed to see documents that relate to me, personally. I was not allowed access to files that might contain the names or details of anybody else, since this could breach data protection laws. And since it would appear that every piece of documentation in the files seemed to include someone else's name, I was not allowed to see anything. Is that clever, or what? I was impressed by how they got around the Freedom of Information Act, but what a manipulation of the law!

We did receive a copy of the doctor's report and x-ray report within a few weeks; which arrived in the same envelope. I opened the envelope and quickly read the reports, expecting to find nothing. Otherwise, why would the social workers not have allowed the magistrates to see them?

I was shocked to find that the doctor's report stated that there was, indeed, bruising to Sally's face. And then, when I read the result of the x-ray report, I felt completely gutted. The report documented an old fracture of the seventh rib and a linear translucency of the upper end of the fibula, which could possibly be a fracture. I held the paper, open-mouthed in shock. A second x-ray had been recommended by the radiologist, but it would appear that this had never taken place.

I was feeling very confused. Could this be true? Could there be a mistake? It seemed, from this, that the injuries to Sally had occurred... but if these reports clearly described the injuries to Sally from when she was a five-week-old baby, why on earth did the social workers prevent the magistrates from seeing the reports? It would have been in their interests to provide such evidence and it would have made their case watertight! The social workers would most certainly have had these reports at the time, and they could have only strengthened their case against Martha. Why would they have fudged the issue in court, and claimed that these reports weren't available for the judge to see, when they had such compelling proof of apparent abuse? It made no sense. I was stunned and bewildered.

It took a while for my head to clear, but then, I read the doctor's report again in its entirety, slowly and methodically. I began to look deeper into the report and not just focus on the bruising, and as I did, a different image began to appear. I did the same with the x-ray report and then, it came to me – the reason why the magistrates could not be allowed to see the reports.

The doctor's report stated: "At the request of the Duty Social Worker, I saw baby Sally and examined her on the afternoon of 12 December 1985. On examination, she was a **clean and healthy baby**; there were **no abnormalities** to be found, other than two bruises. The larger of these was on the left cheek, about 5 cm in diameter and fairly recent. There was also a fading 2 cm bruise over the right eyebrow. In my opinion, both of these would be the result of non-accidental injury." (Author's emphasis, in bold)

Now, considering that Sally had been taken to the doctors by a social worker, who would have told the doctor that this baby had been deserted by her mother in the street, what else could a doctor say, than presume this to be 'non-accidental'? After all, what normal mother would just up and leave her young baby in the street, so social service had to rescue her? The social worker would most definitely not have told the doctor that they had just forcibly removed this five-week-old baby from its mother's arms, in the street.

If you look at how the doctor's letter is laid out, it starts with, "On examination, she was a *clean and healthy baby* with *no abnormalities* to be found" and only finally refers to the bruising. If the bruising had been of serious concern, surely his report would have started by mentioning the bruising? I think we all know that there are bruises and there are bruises! It is easy to see the difference between a deep bruise that a punch from a clenched fist would produce and a superficial or less serious bruise that a poke from a finger might produce. A poke from a social worker's finger in the act of forcibly removing a baby from its mother's arms?

The larger bruise would hardly be the result of beating with a clenched fist, but was likely to be the result of a poke from a finger, during forceful removal in the
street by a social worker. It had been December, and Sally was well dressed for the weather. She had thick, padded clothing and the only part of her body not to be covered was her face. Yes, the more I thought about it, now, I was convinced that the bruise to Sally's face had been inflicted during her removal. It had been distressing and almost violent to witness, and although unintentional, it could have easily misled the doctor.

Now, the x-ray report had been carried out six days after the doctor's examination, which was six days after Sally had been taken from her mother. It describes an old fracture of the left seventh rib and a linear translucency in the region of the upper end of the fibula – her calf bone.

Current thought suggests that, in very young babies, a linear translucency could simply show parts of the bone that have not fully developed, and along with the fracture of the rib apparently older than the baby itself, Sally's were merely defects of birth that correct themselves, given time. If there had been a linear fracture – meaning that the bone had been split down its length, which apparently requires a great amount of force – her leg would have been black and blue with bruising and the baby would have been experiencing horrendous pain. But according to the doctor six days previously, she was a clean and healthy baby!

A second x-ray of an oblique view of this region was recommended by the radiologist, but there is no record of that second x-ray. I am sure the radiologist would have been obliged to take the second x-ray to determine if they had a damaged leg to deal with. Or did the social workers not allow a second x-ray to be taken, for some reason? And if so, why? Did they have power to decree what the hospital could or couldn't do? I wouldn't think so.

My thinking is that the second x-ray would have been taken and shown no fracture. This is why Sally did not need any hospital treatment and was taken straight to foster parents.

So, why was there no trace of a second x-ray? Well, without a conclusive x-ray, the social workers could continue to refer to a *possible* fracture being present. But how could they dispose of an x-ray report altogether, so it was not included in Sally's medical records?

What I also find puzzling is why it took six days after the doctor's examination before Sally was x-rayed. I would have thought the x-ray would have been done immediately after or immediately before the doctor's examination, not six days later.

In my view, the social workers did not show the magistrate the reports because after the social workers had described Sally's injuries, the doctors report should probably have read entirely differently. The magistrates would have expected to read about dirtiness, visible extensive injury and pain; not a clean and healthy baby with no abnormalities to be found, and no hospital treatment needed.

The radiologist's report said the x-ray showed a linear translucency which was *possibly* caused by a fracture and suggested that a second x-ray could confirm or eliminate the presence of a fracture. Because Sally had no bruising to the leg and was not in pain, it would have been obvious that she didn't have a fracture.

By not allowing a second x-ray, the social workers were able to write in their report that the x-ray taken showed 'possible' fractures. They were not telling lies, but they were distorting the details and facts to give a completely false impression to the court on **15 February 1986**. I concluded that this was why the magistrate could not be allowed to see the X-ray and doctor's reports. After they had the care order in place, the social workers could continue to cite Sally's supposed injuries – allegedly inflicted by Martha – as the reason for her removal.

One magistrate was angry enough when she thought the social workers were just plain incompetent! Can you imagine how she'd have reacted if she found out that this clean, healthy baby had been forcibly snatched from its mother in the street? And that the social workers seemed to be falsifying injuries and confessions in an attempt to justify how and why they had taken Sally? The details of how Sally was removed from her mother were never mentioned in court. What do you think the magistrate would have said to that? And what had our solicitor been doing? Not a fat lot!

The only logical explanation for the social workers' vigorous attempts to show that Sally had severe injuries inflicted by violent and bad parents was to cover up their own assault on Martha and their snatching of Sally, both of which were unlawful, in my opinion.

As previously mentioned, Sally applied for copies of her social services files in **April 2013**. I originally thought that they had to comply, by law, within about forty days. I have since discovered that this timeframe applies to virtually all information held on you by anyone – except in the case of records held by social services. They merely have to provide access as soon as they consider it possible, which gives them licence to drag it out for years, if they feel it is necessary to do so.

Why do they have so much power? It was originally intended that social services should protect children, but they seem to use it now to protect themselves.

Sally received several replies apologising for the delay and giving reasons why the files had not yet been made available: staff on holiday, staff off sick, lots of paperwork to go through. All similar excuses to he ones they gave me.

In **April 2014**, a year after her original request, to our amazement, Sally's paperwork arrived.

"I can't believe it, Dad!" Sally cried, grinning, her eyes shining with excitement. And we eagerly fell upon the thick wad of papers.

But to our dismay, it seemed that the authorities had spent those twelve months going over the files, blacking out areas they did not want to show, for whatever reason. It had made the documents almost useless: paragraph after paragraph had been blacked out, and in many cases, a whole page, with the exception of one or two lines, had been obliterated. It made the files nonsensical.

From those documents, I tried to establish how social services had first come to make contact with my family. I have mentioned that as far as I knew, they first came to talk about Martha's bad housing, and yet, this initial contact had resulted in them forcibly removing Sally from her mother!

In these documents, I found: "Reason for referral: ████████████████." Redacted. They were blacked out.

You wait a whole year, and then they send you something unreadable! Should I have expected anything different? Not really. What can you do, when you are up against this sort of thing? They will say it is to protect someone or something, but what happened to the reason for their existence being to protect the child?

During the time of my family's involvement with social services there was little or no access to the Internet, so getting any sort of help or advice was all but impossible, but looking online today and reading similar stories about horrific behaviour by social services towards families and their children, not only in Britain but all over the world, then I think that common sense should tell us that something needs to change. I can understand people's initial reaction to some of the terrible stories that are now coming to light: there must be something wrong with the family or social workers would not be involved in the first place.

Over the years, in talking to close friends and family about our experiences, their common response was: "Aren't there safeguards in place to prevent this sort of thing happening?"

My reply is always: "What good are safeguards, if the people who implement them have gone off the rails?"

Investigations carried out by social workers are intended to be the best safeguards. They are supposed to investigate what is happening with the child, and if something is not how it should be, action needs to be taken – and rightly so.

For example, a social worker goes to the child's school to hear how the child is getting on, because this is one of the most important indicators of a child's well-being. Are the children clean and well fed when they come to school? Do they seem generally happy and mix with others relatively normally? If the answer is yes, there cannot be much wrong with the child. If a child is being abused at home, it will show at school.

Now, what happens when the social worker goes to the child's school to hear what the school has to say, and the school says everything is normal, the children have no problems, they mix well in school and the school has no concerns? Yet, when this information becomes a social worker's report, it reads: "The children are isolated at school. They are delayed in all aspects and the school has serious concerns over the welfare of the children."

This is exactly what happened on one occasion with my family, when the staff at the children's charity family centre tried to prevent me taking the report out of the building. The report stated that the school had all these serious concerns, but when she was shown the report, the school's headmistress said that she had told the social worker the complete opposite: that the school had no concerns whatsoever about the children!

I would like to point out that this is not the same school that Sally attended, where the alleged assault took place – we made sure that the two younger children went to a different school!

When social workers are capable of such a serious distortion of facts, what has happened to the safeguards that are supposed to protect children and their families? They no longer exist, that's what's happened. It is not the system that has failed; it's the people who implement the system who have failed.

How can a problem like this be addressed?

As I described, when a new social worker, Jan Berkley-Grey, was brought onto the case to work with Sally, she said she could see nothing within the family to give her any concerns and she couldn't understand why child protection had taken such a negative view.

Berkley-Grey was removed from the case. As I said previously, when I asked one of the case workers to allow me to contact Berkley-Grey, to seek a positive statement, the social worker told me that I would never be allowed to contact Berkley-Grey for a statement, because it could help my case.

This tells me that the welfare of the children was not the real issue here. A decision had been made by Kathleen Archer, of child protection, to remove the children from the home – and her decision was final. Anyone with a different view to hers was simply taken off the case, even if that person was a fellow social worker.

And what about the children's charity? A supposedly independent organisation whose aim is to help children? They spent over a year writing damning report after damning report for social services, saying how much our bad parenting had damaged the children and that I was unable to accept their concerns. It is impossible not to be bemused by the contradiction in their behaviour. They asserted that we *had* damaged the children, until the children were quickly and unexpectedly taken off the at-risk register, when the charity staff said, "Well, it was obvious all along that there was nothing wrong with the children." If it was so obvious, why had they and social services spent more than two years saying that there was something seriously wrong with the children?

How corrupt does a system have to be? How much damage does it have to cause, before sensible, level-headed people in power can see that something is seriously wrong and decide that things have to change?

In my view, the only way to safeguard against corruption and wrong-doing within social services' child protection system is if social workers are made accountable to the law. When a social worker makes a statement that is obviously false, that worker should face the full weight of the law, just as people in other walks of life have to, if they act in a similar way.

While social workers can say and do as they please in their secret family courts, I see no change being possible.

The historian and politician Lord Acton was famously quoted as saying:

'Power tends to corrupt, and absolute power corrupts absolutely.'

I tell my children we are lucky. We are still here. We are still together (apart from their mother, who lives down the road). We still have our health (apart from their mother, who is still on medication). And, most importantly, we can still laugh (their mother, not so much).

Sometimes they jokingly ask, "Who is the Mega Pig?"

And then they shout, "You are!"

THE END

Worth leaving a review?

If you have read this book, would you consider taking a few minutes to leave a review?

Good, bad or somewhere in between,
your opinion is important,
to me and to the potential future reader.

Thank you.

Websites for your comments:

https://www.amazon.co.uk/Fight-Family-Mega-Pig-File/dp/152298741X

http://www.goodreads.com/book/show/30067030-my-fight-for-my-family

Printed in Poland
by Amazon Fulfillment
Poland Sp. z o.o., Wrocław